THINKING AND WRITING ABOUT

Psychology

Second Edition

Spencer A. Rathus

Harcourt Brace College Publishers

Fort Worth • Philadelphia • San Diego • New York • Orlando • Austin • San Antonio
Toronto • Montreal • London • Sydney • Tokyo

Address for editorial correspondence:
Harcourt Brace College Publishers
301 Commerce Street, Suite 3700
Fort Worth, TX 76102

Address for orders:
Harcourt Brace & Company
6277 Sea Harbor Drive
Orlando, FL 32887-6777
1-800-782-4479 or 1-800-433-0001 (in Florida).

Printed in the United States of America

ISBN: 0-15-504141-X

7 8 9 0 1 2 3 4 5   066   9 8 7 6 5 4 3 2

Contents

Harcourt Brace & Company

This book is primarily intended to stimulate students to think and write about psychology. In doing so, however, this book will also help colleges, professors, and students meet two widespread pedagogical objectives:

1. Critical thinking,
2. Writing across the curriculum.

CRITICAL THINKING

The object of education is to prepare the young to educate themselves throughout their lives.

—Robert M. Hutchins

A great many people think they are thinking when they are merely rearranging their prejudices.

—William James

Most of us take a certain number of 'truths' for granted. One is that authority figures like doctors and government leaders usually provide us with factual information and are generally equipped to make the decisions that affect our lives. But when two doctors disagree as to whether or not surgery is necessary to cure an illness, how can both be correct? We need to rely on ourselves to some degree and to seek the information we need to make our own decisions.

In the fifteenth century it was widely believed that the earth was flat. In the sixteenth century it was widely believed that the sun revolved around the earth. It seems that widely held beliefs are invariably replaced by other widely held beliefs in the fullness of time. It is the hallmark of an educated person to remain skeptical of accepted views and to regard even the most popular beliefs as working assumptions. In the twentieth century, most astronomers widely believe that the universe began with a 'big bang' and has been expanding ever since. It is fascinating to speculate on what views will replace these beliefs tomorrow.

In order to help students evaluate claims, arguments, and widely held beliefs, most colleges today encourage *critical thinking*. Critical thinking has many meanings. On one level, it means taking nothing for granted. It means not believing things just because they are in print or because they were uttered by authority figures or celebrities. It means not necessarily believing that it is healthful to express all of your feelings, even if a friend in analysis urges you to do so. On another level, critical thinking refers to a process of thoughtfully analyzing and probing the questions, statements, and arguments of others. It means examining definitions of terms, examining the premises or assumptions behind arguments, and then scrutinizing the logic with which arguments are developed.

GOALS FOR AN UNDERGRADUATE EDUCATION IN PSYCHOLOGY

Psychologists are working with the Association of American Colleges to establish goals and guidelines for undergraduate education. A psychology task force recently listed nine outcomes or goals for undergraduate education in psychology (McGovern, 1989). The first was to foster a 'knowledge base' consisting of important 'theories, research findings, and issues in psychology.' The second was to promote skills in 'critical thinking and reasoning.' These thinking skills involve:

Development of skepticism about explanations and conclusions
The ability to inquire about causes and effects
Refinement of curiosity about behavior
Knowledge of research methods
The ability to critically analyze arguments

The emphasis on critical thinking reflects the widespread belief that your college education is intended to do more than provide you with a data bank of useful knowledge. It is also meant to provide you with intellectual tools that allow you to learn from and analyze information independently. With these tools, you can continue to educate yourself for the rest of your life.

Colleges nurture academic freedom, so few professors require (or want) students to share and express their own beliefs. By and large, professors are more concerned that students learn how to question and critically examine psychological theory and research, the points of view of other people, and even their own convictions and values. This does not mean that professors insist that students change their beliefs, either. It does mean, however, that professors usually ask students to *support* the views they express in class and in their writing. If students' definitions of terms are muddy, if their premises are shaky, or if their arguments are illogical, professors may encourage other students to challenge them or may personally point out the fallacies in their arguments. Most professors want students to learn to recognize the premises of their arguments, to consider whether they really accept these premises, and to understand whether or not they draw logical conclusions from them.

Some Features of Critical Thinking

This section summarizes some of the principles of critical thinking discussed in Chapter 1 of Rathus' textbooks.

1. **Be skeptical.**

2. **Examine definitions of terms.**

3. **Examine the assumptions or premises of arguments.**

4. **Be cautious in drawing conclusions from evidence.**

5. **Consider alternative interpretations of research evidence.**

6. **Do not oversimplify.**

7. **Do not overgeneralize.**

8. **Apply critical thinking to all areas of life.**

Recognizing Common Fallacies in Arguments

Another aspect of critical thinking is learning to recognize the fallacies in other people's claims and arguments. The following examples of fallacious arguments are discussed in Chapter 1 of Rathus' textbooks.

1. **Arguments Directed to the Person (*Argumentum ad Hominem*)**

2. **Arguments Employing Force (*Argumentum ad Baculum*)**

3. **Appeals to Authority (*Argumentum ad Verecundiam*)**

4. **Appeals to Popularity (*Argumentum ad Populum*)**

As you complete the writing exercises in this book, be skeptical of claims and arguments. Critically examine the evidence presented rather than focusing on the authority, force, or appeal of the people making the argument.

WRITING ACROSS THE CURRICULUM

Books are the carriers of civilization.
—Barbara Tuchman

No man but a blockhead ever wrote except for money.
—Samuel Johnson

I love being a writer. What I can't stand is the paperwork.
—Peter De Vries

Writing is the only thing that, when I do it, I don't feel I should be doing something else.
—Gloria Steinem

'Writing across the curriculum' refers to writing in every subject. You naturally write in an English composition course, and you may be assigned brief or long papers in many other courses. The concept behind writing across the curriculum is that every subject presents an opportunity for expressing yourself in writing and enhancing your writing skills.

Why all this emphasis on writing? Throughout high school and college, many

Harcourt Brace & Company

students have the feeling that compositions and papers are little more than part of the price they have to pay to get a diploma and, eventually, a decent job. They do not see writing as something that is valuable in itself, however.

The fact is that writing is essential, not only in college but also in most professional careers. Business executives need to be able to communicate their ideas through writing. Marketing plans, advertising copy, and proposals for new products must all be fleshed out in words and sentences. Very few lawyers put on courtroom shows like the fabled Perry Mason; most lawyers spend far more time writing contracts and persuasive letters. Technicians, engineers, and scientists have to be able to write precise reports. Think of all the writing that goes into directions for using a stove or a VCR. Consider the detailed writing that is found in armed forces weapons manuals. Engineers and scientists also write technical articles for journals; they review the research in their fields and report on their own research studies. They have to be able to write clearly enough so that other people can follow their directions and arrive at the same results accurately and safely. Doctors, psychologists, counselors, nurses, and dental hygienists must be able to write up reports describing the problems and progress of their patients and clients. Managers of fast-food restaurants write evaluations of employees. Everyone writes business letters of one kind or another—or is inconvenienced if he or she cannot.

Learning how to write also teaches you how to *think*. Part of writing certainly involves proper spelling and usage. In writing, however, you are also forced to organize your ideas and present them logically. Training and practice in writing are therefore also training and practice in thinking.

Writing skills are thus not for college only. Writing skills are not just the province of English teachers, poets, novelists, and journalists. They are for everyone who is receiving an education and contemplating a career.

Many college students fear writing assignments. Many students have not received enough training in high school to make them feel comfortable. Most college instructors of writing see their job as enhancing their students' creativity, critical thinking, and explanatory powers, but not teaching students basic sentence structure and punctuation. Professors in other disciplines often rely completely on short-answer tests to arrive at grades. (They may protest that their job is to teach their subject, not to suffer through their students' incoherent essays and papers.) High-school English teachers sometimes complain that basic skills were not taught in the elementary schools. Elementary school teachers, in turn, often criticize children's home environments for not helping incubate basic writing skills. Writing skills, in short, are valued in college and are essential afterward, but they are taught only by a minority of instructors in a few disciplines.

KINDS OF WRITING

There are many kinds of writing. Writing can be broken down into fiction (imaginary happenings, such as short stories, plays, and novels) and nonfiction (such as directions for assembling machines, essays, theme papers, and term papers). The writing of fiction is usually taught in creative writing courses, although fiction is sometimes assigned in freshman composition classes. Students need not be good at writing fiction to get by in college—unless they're making up excuses as to why they are late with their assignments! By and large, however, college students are required to show or develop some skill at writing nonfiction.

The kinds of nonfiction required of college students are mostly essay answers on tests, theme papers, and term papers. Here we focus on theme papers and research papers, some of which are term papers. A theme is a relatively short paper and is the most common type of paper assigned in courses like freshman composition. There are different kinds of themes, including argument-ative, descriptive, and expository.

The aim of the ***argumentative theme*** is to persuade the reader to adopt a certain point of view. Papers intended to convince the reader that Lady Macbeth was motivated by infertility or that the greenhouse effect will eventually cause persistent droughts in the Midwestern breadbasket are argumentative.

A ***descriptive theme*** paints in words persons, places, or ideas. The infamous 'What I Did on My Summer Vacation' theme is basically descriptive. If you have poetic urges, it is usually best to give vent to them in descriptive themes. Expository themes are explanatory in nature. They are concrete and logically developed.

Expository themes apply to the instructions in your cookbook for concocting guacamole and to laboratory reports. Each discipline (art, biology, physics, psychology, etc.) has its own way of doing things, its own traditions, but they also have some things in common: Explanations are kept as brief and precise as possible. Usually, you explain what you set out to do, why you set out to do it, what you actually did, what you found out, and, sometimes, the implications of what you discovered.

TYPES OF PSYCHOLOGY PAPERS

The types of papers or articles that are printed in psychology journals are examples of expository themes. Three of the most common kinds of expository themes found in the psychological literature are reports of empirical research studies, reviews of the literature on various topics, and theoretical articles.

These papers are most often written in 'APA format.' **APA** stands for American Psychological Association, and the format referred to is the standard for articles that are published in APA journals. Most psychology journals that are not published by the APA also require the APA format.

The APA format is somewhat rigid, but its purpose is to help writers report information clearly and concisely, so that readers may avail themselves of the information without obstacles. Put it another way: the APA format is designed to prevent writers from 'getting in the way' of reporting their research findings or theoretical concepts.

Reports of Empirical Studies

These are reports of original research. Such reports must be to the point (show economy in expression) and broken into standard sections. The usual sections or parts of reports of empirical research studies are:

■ *Introduction* The introduction sets the stage for your research by stating the problem, briefly reviewing previous research in the area, and showing how your research will test or answer some of the issues in the area.

■ *Method* The purpose of this section is to explain what you did so clearly that people reading the report could replicate (duplicate) your work. Describe the subjects or participants, how they were selected for the study, how many actually participated and how many withdrew through the course of the study; the procedures that were used, including the treatments and the equipment; and the methods of assessment that were employed to measure the dependent variables (outcomes). If the details of the treatment or the apparatus are lengthy, you may include them in an appendix at the end of the article or indicate, in a footnote, how the reader may obtain more detailed information.

■ *Results* This section reports your findings.

■ *Discussion* The discussion section usually begins with a brief summary of the previous three sections (preferably one paragraph).

The section then relates the findings to previous research in the area, discusses the implications of the findings for psychological theory, and may suggest directions for future research.

Reviews of the Literature

Rather than report your own original research, literature reviews critically evaluate the previous research in a field of study. The purposes of a review article are to summarize what is known for the reader and to point out the strengths and shortcomings of prior research. Psychology textbooks, such as your introductory psychology textbook, may be considered reviews of the literature in various fields of psychology.

Literature reviews frequently summarize research chronologically—that is, they may be organized according to the sequence of the research in the field and show how new ideas developed out of the testing of older ideas. They may also be organized topically. One section, for example, may review research with human beings, and another section may review

Harcourt Brace & Company

studies with lower animals. Or one section may review correlational studies, and another, experimental research.

Review articles also have introductions and discussion sections.

Theoretical Papers

These papers evaluate and advance psychological theory in the fields of psychology.

In an introductory section, the author will usually state the theoretical problem and summarize much theoretical thinking up to the present day. There may then be a discussion of the shortcomings of current theoretical knowledge. Such shortcomings may involve theoretical contradictions or defects.

It may be pointed out, for example, that some tenets of psychodynamic theory are unscientific because they cannot be *disproved*.

It may be pointed out that the behavior-therapy technique of systematic desensitization is not perfectly behavioral because it relies on mental imagery. Other shortcomings may involve inconsistencies between psychological theory and empirical evidence. The evidence, that is, may contradict the theory. The theory may suggest that increasing motivation enhances performance, but the evidence may show that increasing motivation helps up to a certain point, but then impairs performance.

In a theoretical article, the concluding sections often suggest modifications to the theory that render the theory more logical or more consistent with empirical evidence.

Common Features

Psychology articles also include title pages, abstracts, and references. Your instructor may require that assigned papers also contain these elements, and that they be written in 'APA format.'

■ *Title Page* The title page should include:

- **The title of the paper.** Keep the title as short as possible. The *Publication Manual* of the American Psychological Association suggests that phrases such as

'A Study of' and 'An Experimental Investigation of' are best omitted from the title.
- **The by-line.** The by-line consists of the author's name (or authors' names) and the institution at which the study was conducted (in your case, your college or university).

■ *Abstract* An abstract is a brief summary of the paper's contents. The abstract should immediately inform the reader (or peruser) about the purposes, methods, and findings of the study, although it must be limited to a maximum of 150 words. Because the abstract must pack in a great deal of information into a limited format, it can pose quite a challenge.

Abstracts are used by abstracting and information services to allow scientists who are searching the literature to determine whether or not your article is among the literature they need to review. When writing an abstract, ask yourself whether or not the information you are including would allow another individual to make such a decision.

■ *References* Psychological articles contain only the works that are cited in the article. They are not the same thing as a *bibliography*, which may contain a list of all of the works on a subject (good luck!) or at least a list of all the works which have had an influence on your writing of the article.

The *Publication Manual* of the American Psychological Association notes the following rules for referencing:

- The text of the paper and the list of references must be in agreement. Every study and author in the paper must be referenced in the list, and vice versa.
- References are placed in alphabetical order.
- References to the same authorship are presented chronologically, with the earliest publications listed first.
- References in the text of the paper and in the reference list are written as shown in Table 1 on pages 7–8. Figure 1 on page 9 shows a partial list of references for a psychology article or paper as they would appear at the end of the paper.

Term Papers

Term papers differ from briefer theme papers mainly in length. The paper is called a *term paper* because it is supposed to take a good part of the term to write it, or because it is intended to reflect what you have learned during the term. A term paper in psychology is more likely to be a review of the literature on a subject than to be a report of empirical research.

GUIDELINES FOR GOOD WRITING

Just as no two people are exactly alike (even identical twins have their own private thoughts), no two people write exactly alike. Good writing takes many forms. Some people use slang very well; others fare better when they take a more formal approach. Some writers show strong organizational skills; others have a fine poetic touch and the ability to create vivid images through words. Yet, there are a number of guidelines that hold true for most of us most of the time.

Complete the Assignment

It may not matter how your intelligence and sophistication shine through or how your prose sparkles if you do not follow instructions and carry out the assignment. Make sure that you understand the instructions. If your professor asks for a reaction paper to an essay, make sure that you understand what the professor means by *reaction paper*. Don't hesitate to ask in class; if you are unclear about how to carry out the assignment, other students may be also. If, however, you are concerned that you might take up too much class time, or if you want still more information than can be covered in class, see your instructor during office hours.

If general discussion of the requirements does not create a clear picture for you, ask for examples. You can also ask the instructor to show you one or more models (pieces of writing) that fulfill the assignment.

6

Table 1: Examples of References in APA Format as Found in the Text of a Paper and in the List of References

Reference in Text	Reference in List of References
First citation for two to five authors: (Abramson, Garber, & Seligman, 1980)	Abramson, L. Y., Garber, J., & Seligman, M. E. P. (1980). Learned helplessness in humans: An attributional hypothesis. In G. Garber & M. E. P. Seligman (Eds.), <u>Human helplessness: Theory and application</u>. (pp. 3–34). New York: Academic Press.
Subsequent citations for three or more authors: (Abramson et al., 1980)	[Comments: authors' names are inverted; only initial word (and word following colon) of title of book or chapter of book is capitalized; names of editors are *not* inverted; name of book is underlined (or italicized); pages of chapter are shown as illustrated; editor(s) is/are abbreviated (Ed.) or (Eds.).]
First and subsequent citations for two authors: (Agras, & Kirkley, 1986)	Agras, W. S., & Kirkley, B. G. (1986). Bulimia: Theories of etiology. In K. D. Brownell & J. P. Foreyt (Eds.), <u>Handbook of eating disorders</u>. (pp. 367–378). New York: Basic Books.
First and subsequent citations for two authors: (Ainsworth, & Bowlby, 1991)	Ainsworth, M. D. S., & Bowlby, J. (1991). An ethological approach to personality development. <u>American Psychologist, 46</u>, 333–341. [Comments: only initial word of title of journal or newspaper *article* is capitalized; name of journal is capitalized and underlined (or italicized); volume of journal is underlined (or italicized); page numbers stand alone (without 'p.' or 'pp.').]
First and subsequent citations for one author: (Altman, 1991)	Altman, L. K. (1991, June 18). W.H.O. says 40 million will be infected with AIDS virus by 2000. <u>The New York Times</u>, p. C3. [Comments: newspaper article shows precise date; name of newspaper is capitalized and underlined (or italicized); no volume or issue number is used; page(s) of article is/are preceded by 'p.' or 'pp.']
First and subsequent citations for organization treated as author: (American Psychological Association, 1990)	American Psychological Association. (1990). Ethical principles of psychologists. <u>American Psychologist, 45</u>, 390–395.
First and subsequent citations for six or more authors: (Antoni, et al., 1991)	Listing for six or more authors: Antoni, M. H., et al. (1991). Cognitive-behavioral stress management intervention buffers distress responses and immunologic changes following notification of HIV-1 seropositivity. <u>Journal of Consulting and Clinical Psychology, 59</u>, 906–915.
First and subsequent citations for single author: (Bandura, 1991)	Bandura, A. (1991). Human agency: The rhetoric and the reality. <u>The American Psychologist, 46</u>, 157–162.

Continued on next page

Table 1, Continued

Reference in Text	Reference in List of References
Citation for first article by same authorship in given year: (Baron, 1990a)	Baron, R. A. (1990a). Environmentally induced positive affect: Its impact on self-efficacy, task performance, negotiation, and conflict. <u>Journal of Applied Social Psychology</u>, <u>20</u>, 368–384. [Comment: letter *a* is used to denote reference to first article by the author(s) in a given year.]
Citation for second article by same authorship in given year: (Baron, 1990b)	Baron, R. A. (1990b). Countering the effects of destructive criticism: The relative efficacy of four interventions. <u>Journal of Applied Psychology</u>, <u>75</u>, 235–245. [Comment: letter *b* is used to denote reference to second article by the author(s) in a given year.]
First citation for five or fewer authors: (Beck, Brown, Berchick, Stewart, & Steer, 1990). Subsequent citations for three or more authors: (Beck, et al., 1990).	Beck, A. T., Brown, G., Berchick, R. J., Stewart, B. L., & Steer, R. A. (1990). Relationship between hopelessness and ultimate suicide. <u>American Journal of Psychiatry</u>, <u>147</u>, 190–195.
First and subsequent citations for two authors: (Beck, & Freeman, 1990)	Beck, A. T., & Freeman, A. (1990). <u>Cognitive therapy of personality disorders</u>. New York: Guilford. [Comment: book title is underlined or italicized; only first word of title is capitalized.]
(Beck, & Young, 1985)	Beck, A. T., & Young, J. E. (1985). Depression. In D. H. Barlow (Ed.), <u>Clinical handbook of psychological disorders</u> (pp. 206–244). New York: Guilford Press. [Comment: reference to a chapter in a book edited by one editor.]
(Behrens, 1990)	Behrens, D. (1990, September 21). Test-tube baby in tug-of-war. <u>New York Newsday</u>, pp. 3, 23. [Comment: reference to newspaper article found on nonconsecutive pages.]
(Blakeslee, 1992a)	Blakeslee, S. (1992a, January 7). Scientists unraveling chemistry of dreams. <u>The New York Times</u>, pp. C1, C10. [Comment: Why is the date listed as 1992a?]
(Blakeslee, 1992b)	Blakeslee, S. (1992b, January 22). An epidemic of genital warts raises concern but not alarm. <u>The New York Times</u>, p. C12.

Harcourt Brace & Company

Figure 1:   A Partial List of References Written in the Format Recommended By the American Psychological Association

REFERENCES

Abraham, L. K. (1993). Mama might be better off dead: The failure of health care in urban America. Chicago: University of Chicago Press.

Abramson, L. Y., Garber, J., & Seligman, M. E. P. (1980). Learned helplessness in humans: An attributional hypothesis. In G. Garber & M. E. P. Seligman (Eds.), Human helplessness: Theory and application. (pp. 3–34). New York: Academic Press.

Ader, D. N., & Johnson, S. B. (1994). Sample description, reporting, and analysis of sex in psychological research: A look at APA and APA division journals in 1990. American Psychologist, 49, 216–218.

Agras, W. S., & Kirkley, B. G. (1986). Bulimia: Theories of etiology. In K. D. Brownell & J. P. Foreyt (Eds.), Handbook of eating disorders. (pp. 367–378). New York: Basic Books.

Ainsworth, M. D. S., & Bowlby, J. (1991). An ethological approach to personality development. American Psychologist, 46, 333–341.

Aldag, R. J., & Fuller, S. R. (1993). Beyond fiasco: A reappraisal of the groupthink phenomenon and a new model of group decision processes. Psychological Bulletin, 113, 533–552.

Altman, L. K. (1991, June 18). W.H.O. says 40 million will be infected with AIDS virus by 2000. The New York Times, p. C3.

American Psychological Association. (1990). Ethical principles of psychologists. American Psychologist, 45, 390–395.

Antoni, M. H., et al. (1991). Cognitive-behavioral stress management intervention buffers distress responses and immunologic changes following notification of HIV-1 seropositivity. Journal of Consulting and Clinical Psychology, 59, 906–915.

Bandura, A. (1991). Human agency: The rhetoric and the reality. The American Psychologist, 46, 157–162.

Baron, R. A. (1990a). Environmentally induced positive affect: Its impact on self-efficacy, task performance, negotiation, and conflict. Journal of Applied Social Psychology, 20, 368–384.

Baron, R. A. (1990b). Countering the effects of destructive criticism: The relative efficacy of four interventions. Journal of Applied Psychology, 75, 235–245.

Beck, A. T., Brown, G., Berchick, R. J., Stewart, B. L., & Steer, R. A. (1990). Relationship between hopelessness and ultimate suicide. American Journal of Psychiatry, 147, 190–195.

Beck, A. T., & Freeman, A. (1990). Cognitive therapy of personality disorders. New York: Guilford.

Beck, A. T., & Young, J. E. (1985). Depression. In D. H. Barlow (Ed.), Clinical handbook of psychological disorders (pp. 206–244). New York: Guilford Press.

Behrens, D. (1990, September 21). Test-tube baby in tug-of-war. New York Newsday, pp. 3, 23.

Blakeslee, S. (1992a, January 7). Scientists unraveling chemistry of dreams. The New York Times, pp. C1, C10.

Blakeslee, S. (1992b, January 22). An epidemic of genital warts raises concern but not alarm. The New York Times, p. C12.

Blakeslee, S. (1994, April 13). Black smokers' higher risk of cancer may be genetic. The New York Times, p. C14.

Write for Your Audience

If you are writing a children's story, keep the vocabulary simple and the sentences short. If you are writing an argumentative theme to persuade pro-choice people that abortion is morally wrong, don't begin with, 'Abortion is murder and people who support abortion are murderers.' All you will accomplish is to alienate your audience. Instead, write something like, 'Abortion is a complex and troubling issue to most of us, and people on all sides of the issue share deep, sincere convictions.' In this way, you recognize your audience's earnestness and get them involved. You can develop your particular viewpoints later.

If you are writing a journal article for professional colleagues, follow APA guidelines to the letter. Be concise, clear, and organized.

Write Clearly and Simply

Most good writing is reasonably easy to read. Don't have the idea that intelligent writing has to be hard to follow, like a Henry James novel or a Shakespearean play. Unless your assignment is to write a Victorian novel or an Elizabethan play, don't try to manufacture an intricate style or several layers of meaning.

The APA *Publication Manual* advises you to present your ideas in a logical order, express them smoothly, and choose your words carefully. Below are examples of writing that lack clarity and simplicity, and of changes that make the examples clearer, simpler, and at least a bit better.

AWFUL	BETTER
Psychologists have engaged in complex correlational studies among peoples of diverse cultural subgroups to ascertain whether or not various variables related to the types of stimulation received in the home have effects on children's performance on intelligence tests and in the school.	Psychologists have correlated features of the home environment with the IQ scores and achievements of children from diverse ethnic groups.
Tyrants may arrive at the point where the recipients of their despotism are no longer swayed by their inhumanity.	People may lose their fear of tyrants.
In your writing, it is a good idea to keep your sentences as simple as you can reasonably do.	Keep sentences simple.
There are many different views and controversies surrounding the ethical nature of punishment and its effects on children's behavior in the school setting.	There is controversy concerning the ethics and efficacy of punishment in the school setting.

Harcourt Brace & Company

Be Willing to Make Mistakes

> Failure is the condiment that gives success its flavor.
>
> —Truman Capote

No college student is a perfect writer. Everyone makes mistakes. If you didn't make mistakes, you would not need an education.

The point is to learn from your errors. When some aspect of a writing exercise is marked as poor, or wrong, make sure that you understand why. If you do not, you may repeat the mistake.

Keep a Notebook or a Journal

Creative writers, journalism students, and English majors are encouraged to keep notebooks to jot down important thoughts as they occur.

Sometimes they record the events around them–the heavy sky that threatens to burst into a storm or the suspended animation of a frozen January hillside; at other times they record their inmost thoughts and feelings.

As a psychology student, you may wish to keep a journal in which you note people's behavior (and apparent mental processes) under various circumstances. You may wish to note how you and other people respond to stress, to feeling that you are 'in love,' or to a film or a TV show. You may jot down examples of conditions that make it easier for your to learn or remember academic material. Consider your motives for doing things and your responses to your successes and failures. You may also jot down potential psychological research studies that occur to you.

Determine the Length of a Paper Logically

Students are perpetually concerned about how long a paper should be. The correct answer is simple in principle, but it leaves many students dissatisfied. Generally speaking, the right number of words is the minimal number of words it takes to do the job. Let me note again that the APA *Publication Manual* urges frugality with words–'economy of expression.'

Put it another way: Everything else being equal, a briefer paper or research report is better than a longer paper.

If you're not sure how long a paper should be, ask the professor or check out previous papers that earned high grades. If the professor is not specific about numbers of words or pages, perhaps she or he can give you an impression of how long it should take to write the paper. Is it a paper that you ought to be able to write in one afternoon or evening? Perhaps that would be two to five pages long (typed, double-spaced). Is it a term paper that requires a few days of library work and a few more days of writing? If so, 20 to 30 typewritten, double-spaced pages (including footnotes and bibliography) might be in order.

In any case, if the instructor specifies the number of pages for an assignment, be sure to comply. Failure to do so, even by a few pages in one direction or another, can result in a lower grade.

Avoid Plagiarism

> I found your essay to be good and original. However, the part that was original was not good and the part that was good was not original.
>
> —Samuel Johnson

Plagiarism derives from the Latin *plagiarius*, which roughly translates as 'kidnapper' in English. Plagiarism is literary theft–the stealing of another person's ideas or words and passing them off as your own.

Let's be honest. (Can we talk here?) Some students intentionally steal the work of others. They pass off a paper that was written by a fraternity brother eight years ago as their own, or they copy passages of books verbatim. Students are not the only plagiarists. New reports now and then carry charges of plagiarism by film script writers or politicians. I have even known architecture students to steal designs from magazines.

Other students plagiarize inadvertently, however. The penalties for plagiarism can be severe. Failing the paper is a minimal penalty; plagiarizers can also fail the course. Now and then, students are pressured to withdraw from college as a result of plagiarism. Stiff penalties seem appropriate for purposeful plagiarism. It is a pity to suffer them, however, for accidental plagiarism.

Professors may not be able to determine whether students have adapted or copied the papers of other students. It is relatively easy, however, for professors to discern passages that have been taken whole from books or articles. The passage may show a level of literary sophistication that exceeds that of the great majority of students. There may be a cogent recounting of facts that could be created only by an expert in the field. There may also be obvious inconsistencies in the paper: The student's own writing may struggle for clarity, while pilfered passages shine through.

The following guidelines will enable you to avoid the pitfalls and penalties of plagiarism.

1. When you mention other people's ideas or theories, attribute the ideas to their proper source. Write, for example,

   Abnormal behavior affects everyone in one way or another (Rathus & Nevid, 1991). If we confine our definition of abnormal behavior to traditional psychological disorders–anxiety, depression, schizophrenia, abuse of alcohol and other drugs, and the like–perhaps one in three of us have been affected (Robins et al., 1984). If we include sexual dysfunctions and difficulties adjusting to the demands of adult life, many more are added. If we extend our definition to include malad-aptive or self-defeating behavior patterns like compulsive gambling and dependence on nicotine, a clear majority of us are affected (Rathus & Nevid, 1991).

2. When you use other people's words, either place them in quotation marks or indent the material. Let length be your guide. When a passage runs from a few words to about four lines, use quotation marks. If a passage runs to five or more lines, indent the material similarly to the way I indented the preceding material on abnormal behavior. Whether you use quotation marks or indent, note the source of the material, including the page or pages on which it is found.

3. You can usually use a brief string (say two or three words) of your source's writing without quotation marks. Use quotation marks, however, if one of the words is a technical term or shows a fine literary turn of phrase–something you might not have arrived at on your own.

4. Hold on to the outline (if you used one) and the working drafts of your paper. If you are falsely accused of plagiarism, you can trace the development of your ideas and your phrasing.

Pick a Topic

You say there is nothing to write about. Then write to me that there is nothing to write about.

—Pliny the Younger

There are no dull subjects. There are only dull writers.

—H. L. Mencken

Professors may assign concrete topics, such as a reaction to a piece of writing, or they may provide a list of topics from which you must choose. Sometimes professors purposefully leave topics wide open. Professors may also assign a paper on some aspect of a topic, which tends to leave the decision pretty much to the student.

There are no hard-and-fast rules to picking a topic. By and large, however, writers–including college students–tend to be at their best on subjects with which they are familiar. Let us consider some motives for picking topics and ways to make them manageable.

Write About Things You Know About

I should not talk so much about myself if there were anybody else whom I knew as well.

—Henry David Thoreau

The first novels of writers tend to be autobiographic. This is true, in part, because writers seek ways of expressing their own ideas and making sense out of their own experiences. It is also true because it is helpful to write about things you know about. When you write about things you know about, you can devote more of your energies to the writing itself and relatively

Harcourt Brace & Company

less to research. Also, we tend to think more deeply and critically about things with which we are familiar. Everything else being equal, essays about the familiar may impress the instructor as more sophisticated than essays about unfamiliar topics.

Write About Things That Interest You

> The best way to become acquainted with a subject is to write a book about it.
> —Benjamin Disraeli

Another motive for writing is to help you learn and organize your thoughts about an interesting topic. Return to the abortion issue. You may have strong ideas about abortion but little or no knowledge of the legal issues involved or the history of pro-life and pro-choice movements. You could thus focus on historic and legal issues as a way of expanding your knowledge of the subject.

Perhaps you are intrigued by environmental psychology. Consider environmental issues such as acid rain or the greenhouse effect. You may have heard that Earth is undergoing a warming trend (greenhouse effect) because of certain emissions, but you may have little or no idea about what emissions are. You could write a paper on the greenhouse effect as a way of becoming familiar with the atmospheric effects of various chemicals, the sources of these chemicals, and scientific and political efforts to control their emission.

Delimit the Topic

There is usually no magical fit between a topic and a theme paper of, say, 400 words or a term paper of 25 typewritten pages. By and large, you must make the topic fit. Although you may sometimes be at a loss for words, it may be easier to expand an apparently small topic to term-paper size than to cut a broad topic down to size.

Are you interested in writing a paper on the 'nature' of motivation? (If so, perhaps you should take out an insurance policy that protects you from sheer exhaustion.)

As a first step, you could choose between papers on, say, general theories of motivation, a paper that reviews theories of topics in motivation (such as a paper on theories of hunger, theories of thirst, or theories of homosexuality), or a paper that is limited to a more circumscribed area within a topic (such as the effects of the contemporary image of the ideal female figure on eating disorders). The last topic could be delimited further to address anorexia nervosa only.

If you find that there is too much literature to cover for a brief assignment, you may 'trim' a topic on general theories of motivation to contemporary cognitive theories of aggression. In so doing, you delimit general theories to contemporary cognitive theory, and you delimit motivation to one area of motivated behavior–aggression.

Write a Thesis Statement

If you are writing an argumentative theme paper, it is helpful to clarify your purpose through a thesis statement. A thesis is a proposition that is maintained or defended in an argument. Once you have narrowed your topic, try to express the thesis of your paper as briefly as possible–in a single sentence, if you can. You don't have to include the thesis statement in your paper. Instead, you can pin it up on the wall and use it as a guide in writing. A thesis statement helps keep you from straying; it channels your arguments and evidence toward a goal.

If you are writing about abortion, for example, your thesis statement could be 'Abortion is the taking of a human life,' or 'The individual woman has a right to exercise control over the events occurring inside her body.' If you are writing about the effects of the contemporary image of the ideal female figure on eating disorders, your thesis statement could be 'Contemporary images of women in the media are connected with a vast increase in the incidence of anorexia nervosa.'

Don't Wait for Inspiration–Get Going!

> 'Where shall I begin, please your Majesty?' he asked.

'Begin at the beginning,' the King said, gravely, 'and go on till you come to the end: then stop.'
—Lewis Carroll, *Alice in Wonderland*

The idea is to get the pencil moving quickly.
—Bernard Malamud

The idea of getting going is not elementary or silly, even if it sounds so. Many students bog down soon after they select a topic. (So do many professional writers!)

Getting going can mean going to the library and beginning to research the topic. Getting going can mean making an outline. Getting going can mean following inspiration and jotting down the introduction, some of the conclusions, or some of the ideas that you will probably use in the body of the paper. You can write down ideas on index cards or on loose-leaf pages that you reorder later on. If you are using word-processing, can save random thoughts in separate files and integrate them later. You can also save them in the same file and then move them around as blocks of text later on.

The point is this: You've got to get going somewhere and at some time. If you have no plan at all, spend a few minutes to formulate a plan. If you have a plan and some useful thoughts come to you, feel free to stray from the plan and jot these thoughts down. It is easier to return to a plan than to reconstruct moments of inspiration!

For most of us, writing, like invention, is 10 percent inspiration and 90 percent perspiration. You cannot force inspiration. You can only set the stage for inspiration by delving into your topic–perhaps by formulating a plan (e.g., beginning with library work), perhaps by writing an outline, perhaps by talking with other people about the topic. Then, when inspiration strikes, jot it down. Keep this in mind, too: A good paper does not have to be inspired. A good paper can address the topic in a coherent, useful way without bursts of genius, without poetry. In fact, if you adhere to the recommendations in the APA *Publication Manual*, poetry is largely out of fashion.

Make an Outline

With nearly any kind of writing, it is helpful to make an outline. Short stories and novels profit from outlines of their plots and characters. Essays, even brief essays of the sort you may write on a test, profit from a listing of the issues to be raised or topics to be covered. With term papers, most students find it essential not only to list the topics that are to be covered, but also to sketch out how they will be covered.

Outlines usually take the following form:

```
I. Major head
   A. Second-level head
   B. Second-level head
      1. Third-level head
         a. Fourth-level head
         b. Fourth-level head
      2. Third-level head
```

Psychology articles have introductions, methods sections, results, and discussion sections. Theme papers and term papers have beginnings (introductions), middles (bodies), and ends (conclusions). In writing theme papers and term papers, students can use a major head for the paper's introduction, one or more major heads for the body of the paper, and another major head for the conclusion.

You are now taking an introductory psychology course. In the future you may take a developmental psychology course, a human sexuality course, or a health course. In any of them, you might be writing a term paper on ways of coping with infertility. Your outline could look something like Figure 2 on page 16.

Compose a Draft

A draft is a rough or preliminary sketch of a piece of writing. One way to write a draft of an article, theme paper, or term paper is to flesh out an outline of the paper. Another is to start writing the sections you know most about, or have the strongest feelings about, and then assemble them like a puzzle. Still another is to just start writing, without even a mental outline, and somehow to arrive at what seems to be a completed work.

Let's assume that you are using an outline and consider, in Figure 2 on page 16, how you might flesh it out, section by section.

Harcourt Brace & Company

Introduction to the Paper

> If you can't annoy somebody, there's little point in writing.
>
> —Kingsley Amis

The introduction to a psychology article states the problem, briefly reviews previous research in the area, and shows how your research or theoretical discussion will test or answer some of the issues in the area.

The introduction to a theme paper or a term paper also has similar functions. It presents a number of the issues you will discuss, but it may also aim to arouse the interest of the reader (and the instructor!). You may want to include your thesis statement somewhere in the introduction (that is, 'It will be shown that. . .'), but it is not necessary. If you are going to wax poetic in a paper, the beginning is as good a place as any. Here are just a handful of the ways in which writers grab the reader's interest:

1. Use an anecdote (as with the plight of Maggie).

2. Use an interesting piece of information from within the paper (e.g., 'One American couple in six cannot conceive a child.')

3. Couple a fact with irony (for example, 'Despite the concern of environmentalists that we are witnessing a population explosion, one American couple in six cannot conceive a child.' Or, 'In an era when we are inundated with news about the high incidence of teenage pregnancy, one American couple in six cannot conceive a child.')

4. Use a quote from literature (for example, 'In Genesis 3:16 it is written, 'In sorrow thou shalt bring forth children.' Sad to say, it is the sorrow of one American couple in six that they shall *not* be able to bring forth children.' This example combines a Biblical quote, irony, and a play on words–that is, the double use of the word *sorrow* and pointing out that so many parents will *not* bear ['bring forth'] children.).

5. Use a rhetorical question ('Did you know that one American couple in six cannot conceive a child?' Or, 'Did you know that many couples who delay marriage and childbearing in an effort to establish careers are playing Russian roulette with fertility?'). A so-called rhetorical question is not really meant to be answered. It is intended as an attention-grabbing way of leading into a topic.

You can also leave the writing of the important beginning lines of the paper until the end, when you have a greater grasp of the subject and are more acquainted with the issues involved. Of course, you are free to jot down notes about possible beginnings as you work on other parts of the paper–whenever inspiration strikes.

Then the introduction can go on to explain the issues that will be covered in the paper and how the paper will approach the topic.

Figure 2:   Partial Outline for Term Paper on 'Ways of Coping with Infertility'

```
  I. Introduction
     A. Attention getter (Maggie's story)
     B. Extent of the problem
     C. What I will do in this paper
 II. Sources of infertility
     A. Problems that affect the male
        1. Low sperm count
        2. Irregularly shaped sperm
        3. Low sperm motility
        4. Infectious diseases
        5. Trauma or injury
        6. Auto-immune response
     B. Problems that affect the female
        1. Lack of ovulation
           a. Hormonal irregularities
           b. Malnutrition
           c. Stress
        2. Obstructions or malfunctions of the reproductive tract
        3. Endometriosis
           a. Special problems of 'yuppies'
III. Methods for Overcoming Infertility
     A. Methods for overcoming male fertility problems
        1. Methods for overcoming low sperm count
           a. Artificial insemination
        Etc.
     B. Methods for overcoming female fertility problems
        1. Methods for overcoming lack of ovulation
        2. Methods for overcoming obstructions or malformations
           a. In vitro fertilization
           b. Gamete intrafallopian transfer (GIFT)
           c. Zygote intrafallopian transfer (ZIFT)
           d. Donor IVF
           e. Embryonic transfer
           f. Surrogate motherhood
        3. Methods for overcoming endometriosis
 IV. Psychological Issues
  V. Financial Issues
 VI. Legal/Moral Issues
VII. Conclusions
     A. Brief review (summary)
     B. Conclusions (points to be made)
     C. Future questions or directions
```

Harcourt Brace & Company

Body of the Paper The body of the paper is the meat of the paper. If you are criticizing a work of literature, a film, or an art exhibit, this is where you list the strengths and weaknesses of the work and support your views. If you are writing an argumentative theme, this is where you state your premises and explain your logic. If you are reviewing research, this is where you explain who did what, when, and how. If your paper explains a number of processes (for example, methods for overcoming infertility), this is where you get down to their nuts and bolts.

In the body of the paper, you paint in the details. If you are writing the term paper on infertility, in section II (according to your outline), you describe endometriosis and explore theories as to how endometriosis impairs fertility. In section VI, you may point out that surrogate mothers are the actual biological mothers of the children who are born to them, and that courts are in conflict as to whether biological mothers can sign away their rights to their children. You could expand your coverage by exploring religious opinions on surrogate motherhood and other issues and devoting space to the psychological and legal ramifications of the celebrated Mary Beth Whitehead case.

Sometimes it seems that subject matter must be organized in a certain way. At other times, organization may appear more flexible. In the paper on infertility, the body began with a section on sources of infertility. There was then a section on methods of overcoming infertility, followed by sections on psychological and related issues. The body of the paper could also have been organized according to kinds of problems. Section II could have been labeled 'Problems That Affect the Male.' Subsection 1 of section II could still have discussed low sperm count. Sections within subsection 1, however, could have discussed (a) sources of low sperm count, (b) methods of overcoming low sperm count, and (c) psychological and (d) other issues involved in handling the problem in the prescribed ways. Section III could then have discussed problems that affect the female.

Conclusion of the Paper The conclusion or discussion section of a paper may contain more than conclusions. Like the introduction, the conclusion has many functions. The introduction of a paper tells readers where they're going. The conclusion tells them where they've been.

In the paper on infertility, the last part of your introduction tells readers where they're going. In the sample outline, the first part of the conclusion tells readers where they've been. The first part of the discussion or concluding section is an excellent place for summarizing or briefly reviewing the information presented in the body. In summarizing the body, you are not simply adding words–that is, 'padding' to meet a length requirement. You are reminding the reader of the major points as a way of leading up to your judgments, inferences, or opinions.

Then you may arrive at the conclusions themselves. Your conclusions put everything together. They explain what it all means. One conclusion of the paper on infertility could be that science is continually finding innovative ways of overcoming fertility problems. Another conclusion could be that these innovations have created new ethical and religious dilemmas. You could also take a personal ethical or religious stance, assuming that you label it as your view and do not equate it with eternal truth or majority opinion. Still another conclusion could be that certain aspects of modern life (for example, toxins, delay of childbearing) contribute to infertility.

Ideally, the conclusion section ends with a bang. The beginning of a paper may attempt to grab the reader's interest, and the ending sometimes also aims to achieve an impact. You can refer to future directions–perhaps the possibility that someday it may be possible to create a child by processing nearly any cell from the father and any cell from the mother. You can go for shock value with the notion that the parents could conceivably be of the same gender, or that there might be only one parent (as in cloning). You can return to Maggie's suffering and suggest that would-be parents will no longer have to undergo her travails.

You can also speculate on how reproductive technology may have a wide impact on social, religious, and political institutions. In a more matter-of-fact mode, you can suggest new avenues of research. You can also use humor, irony, or rhetorical questions–the same devices that draw readers into papers.

The first few lines of the paper make your first impression. The last few lines make your final impression. These are the places where you want to make the greatest impact. If there are sentences you are going to work, work, and rework, let them be the first and last few sentences of the paper.

A CLOSER LOOK

Overcoming a Writing Block

Ah, that blank sheet of paper! The possibilities are endless, so why can't you get something down?

All writers, not just college students, find themselves staring at that empty page now and then, wondering how to overcome a 'writing blocks.'

Imagine that you have picked a topic and have been staring at the page for half an hour. Nothing is coming to mind. What can you do? There are no certain answers, but here are some suggestions that have helped other students.

1. **Brainstorm.** In brainstorming, you do not try to narrow in on a single way to solve a problem. Instead, you generate as many kinds of approaches as possible. Set a time limit for your brainstorming. Then sit back and allow any relevant ideas to pop into mind, even outlandish ideas. Or ask roommates and friends for their ideas–even silly ones. During the session, just record ideas; don't judge them. When the session is finished, consider each idea and test those that seem most likely to be of help.

2. **Take a break.** Have a snack, call a friend, take a shower, get on the rowing machine. Then get back to work. You may find that your ideas have incubated while you were taking your break. When we stand back from the problem for a while, a solution may later appear to us.

3. **Work on another assignment.** Instead of continuing to frustrate yourself, complete another assignment. Then return to the paper refreshed.

4. **Force yourself to write.** Make yourself write on the subject for a specific amount of time–say, for 20 minutes. Try to develop the arguments in the paper. Then critically examine what you have written.

5. **Switch tools.** If you've been processing words on a personal computer, try a typewriter for a while. Or use longhand.

6. **Skip to another section.** Work on another section of the paper. Type up the reference list, for instance. (It's amazing how reviewing sources helps generate ideas!) Or work on your 'dynamite' opening paragraph.

7. **Let the paper go for a few days.** This alternative may help when a short break is ineffective and you still have plenty of time to complete the paper.

8. **Check with the instructor.** He or she may have some excellent advice for resuming the paper. Some instructors do not mind offering detailed suggestions.

9. **Copy and go!** Copy the last sentence or paragraph you wrote and just go with it! Or sketch four or five different directions you can take.

10. **Accept reality?** Sometimes you can't go on because your ideas are truly at a dead end. If the block persists, consider tossing out what you have written and starting from scratch. Perhaps you should change topics. If you have already written 20 pages or checked 50 sources, however, you may find it worthwhile to explore switching topics with your instructor before chucking it into the circular file (that is, the wastebasket).

Harcourt Brace & Company

Revise the Paper

It's none of their business that you have to learn how to write. Let them think you were born that way.

—Ernest Hemingway

I can't write five words but that I change seven.

—Dorothy Parker

Read over your compositions and, when you meet a passage which you think is particularly fine, strike it out.

—Samuel Johnson

Wolfgang Amadeus Mozart is the great musician who bridged the Baroque and Romantic movements. His musical compositions are distinctive not only for their majesty, but also because they were composed practically without revision. It is as though his original conception of his music was complete and flawless. He is a rarity in the world of music.

It is also rare in the world of writing that our original ideas are complete and flawless. There are many false starts, many bad passages. Good writing usually requires revision, sometimes many revisions, even when the writer is experienced. Revision is a natural part of the writing process. Frequently, revision spells the difference between a paper that deserves an F and one that earns an A.

On the other hand, papers should not be revised just for the sake of revision. Now and then we may produce a first draft that we cannot improve. When this occurs, an old saying applies: 'If it ain't broke, don't fix it.'

There are revisions, and then there are revisions. Rarely is every sentence or even every section of a paper revised. Sometimes we revise papers in order to fine-tune our prose, to improve our sentence structure, to reconsider our choice of words. This type of revising is referred to as *editing*.

Editing involves scrutinizing the paper word by word and changing anything that looks wrong, weak, or inappropriate. Editing extends to replacing words, sentences, and paragraphs with improved versions.

Sometimes we revise in order to reshape our ideas so that they fit together more coherently. At other times, we revise to fill gaps. At still other times, we labor to perfect our beginnings and endings.

How much revision is enough? That depends on you as a writer, on the piece that you are writing, and on the expectations of your instructors. As you move more deeply into your college career, you will gain a more accurate impression of how much revision your work usually requires to satisfy your professors–and yourself.

Here are some specific suggestions for revising your papers:

1. **Create distance between you and your work.** Sometimes you need a bit of distance between yourself and your work to recognize weaknesses and errors. One good way to create this distance is to let time pass between drafts—at least a day. In this way, you may be able to look at certain passages or ideas from a new perspective. Of course, you cannot use this method if you don't begin a term paper until a few days before it is due! Another method is to have a trusted friend, family member, or tutor at the college learning center look over the paper. Then you must try to listen to suggestions with an unbiased ear.

2. **Check the draft against the outline.** Are there obvious omissions? Have you strayed from the topic?

3. **Place earlier drafts beside you as you write.** Start writing from scratch, but follow the earlier versions as you proceed. Use segments of earlier versions that seem right. Omit sections that are weak or incorrect.

4. **Set aside earlier drafts and sketch a new version.** Then compare the sketch with earlier drafts, and incorporate the strengths of each version.

5. **Read the draft aloud.** When we listen to ourselves, we sometimes gain a new

perspective on what we are saying–or not saying. This is another way to create a bit of distance between our writing and ourselves. You can also try reading the paper aloud to a friend.

6. **Try a new direction.** If something isn't working, consider taking a different approach. It is not unusual, for example, to change a thesis statement after completing a draft of a paper. Or you could find that you need to check out a different kind of research.

7. **Drop passages that do not work.** This may be the hardest piece of advice to follow. It is painful to throw a piece of work into the wastebasket, especially if we have devoted hours to it. Yet, not every effort is of high quality. *One of the important differences between artists and hacks is that the former are more willing to acknowledge their failures and to toss them onto the scrap heap.*

8. **Ask the instructor for advice.** Drop by during office hours and share some of your concerns with the instructor. You help organize your own thoughts and show respect for the instructor's time when you preplan your questions and make them fairly concrete. Don't say, 'I think something's wrong with my paper, but I don't know what.' Say, instead, 'My thesis was A, but the research seems to be showing B. Should I modify the thesis? Have I hit the right research?' By asking the instructor for advice, you do not appear weak and dependent. Instead, you appear sincere and interested in self-improvement. This is precisely the attitude that your instructor respects.

Using a Word Processor Professor Jacqueline Berke at Drew University notes that because of word processing,

'[Our] understanding of the way people write–the stages–the process–has changed. The phase of writing that is actually most important is revision. Yet how much time does the poor student give to revision?' She remembers a comment from a student's journal: 'The computer makes revision a playground instead of a punishment' (Boyer, 1987, pp. 171—172).

A good word-processing program can help you in many ways:

1. The single greatest advantage to word processing is that you can edit a manuscript indefinitely without having erasures, arrows, and scrawls between the lines. With every change, the material on the screen is brand new. The actual mechanics of making changes are relatively effortless and do not compromise your wish to achieve perfection.

2. You can save each draft of a paper for future reference. For example, in the paper on infertility, the outline could be saved as

   INFERT.OUT

   The first draft could be saved as:

   INFERT.D1

   Subsequent drafts can be numbered. Students should always make and keep copies of the papers they submit. When you use word processing, you save your papers electronically on fixed disks or floppy disks. Each copy of the paper is an original (called a 'hard copy' or a 'display copy'), and you can generate as many original copies as you like.

3. In case the question arises as to whether your paper is original, or written by you, copies of each working draft can be produced in evidence.

4. You can save related thoughts or abstracts of research studies in separate files and integrate them later on.

5. Many word-processing programs automatically renumber all footnotes or endnotes when you insert a new entry.

Harcourt Brace & Company

6. Many word-processing programs check the spelling for you. Such programs catch the following errors:

> I shall show that Woody Allen's recent <u>tradegies</u> are less <u>successfull</u> than his early comedies as works of art.

Spell-checking programs do not catch errors such as the following, however:

> I shall show <u>than</u> Woody Allen's recent tragedies <u>art</u> less <u>successfully that</u> his early comedies as <u>words on</u> art.

7. Many word-processing programs have thesauruses that allow you to search for better wording conveniently.

Proofread the Paper

> A man occupied with public or other important business cannot, and need not, attend to spelling.
> —Napoleon Bonaparte

> I know not, madam, that you have a right, upon moral principles, to make your readers suffer so much.
> —Samuel Johnson, letter to Mrs. Sheridan, after publication of her novel in 1763

> This is the sort of English up with which I will not put.
> —Sir Winston Churchill

Napoleon was probably powerful enough, of course, that few would have brought misspellings to his attention. Most of us do not have the prerogatives of Napoleon. Proofreading is intended to catch the kinds of errors that make many professors groan and, in Johnson's words, 'suffer so much.' Proofreading is a form of editing directed at catching errors in spelling, usage, and punctuation, instead of enhancing the substance of the paper. Proofreading is not generally a creative process; it is more mechanical. On the other hand, if in proofreading you discover that a word does not accurately express your intended meaning, a bit of creativity might be needed in order to replace it or recast the sentence.

Importance of Proofreading

> I will not go down to posterity talking bad grammar.
> —Benjamin Disraeli (Correcting one of his manuscripts on his deathbed)

For a largely mechanical process, proofreading is extremely important. For example, poor spelling and sentence structure suggest ignorance. Whether or not the instructor states that attention will be paid to spelling and so forth, you may still be judged by the mechanics. That is, an instructor who believes that you cannot spell may also believe that you cannot write a good paper.

When a paper has mechanical errors, the message to the instructor is very clear: You don't care enough to proofread the paper yourself or to have it proofread by someone who knows the mechanics.

Many campuses have tutorial centers at which you can have your papers proofread without charge. You may have a variety of reasons for not using the tutorial service: unwillingness to have your work scrutinized by someone else (but your instructor will scrutinize it, anyway); lack of time or inconvenient location (which is more inconvenient in the long run: writing the paper in time to have it proofread, or receiving a poorer grade than necessary?); or simply not caring.

Whatever your reason for failing to proofread your paper, your instructor will interpret the flaws as signs of (1) lack of knowledge and (2) not caring—leading to lack of effort. Lack of knowledge and lack of effort are the two major reasons for poor grades on papers.

On the other hand, don't expect a proofreader to catch every error. Most tutors, for example, point out errors but do not make corrections themselves. Moreover, having a tutor check your paper does *not* remove your responsibility for catching and correcting errors. Nor does it guarantee that all errors have been highlighted. So don't blame your tutor for your own errors. The best way to work with a tutor is to have him or her read over your paper and make suggestions at various stages of the paper's development. You should also be striving to learn rules for proper usage—not just to catch the errors in a single paper.

Tips for Proofreading The following guidelines will help you proofread successfully:

1. When proofreading, read your paper letter by letter, word by word, phrase by phrase, punctuation mark by punctuation mark. (Some English professors recommend starting at the end of your paper and reading it backwards sentence by sentence as a way of catching small errors.) Don't focus on issues such as poetic value and persuasiveness of arguments. Pay attention to the littlest things. Are you using slang words to add color and help make your arguments, or are you just careless?

2. Check as to whether your tenses are consistent. Are you saying Are you saying 'Tolman *noted* (past tense) that...' in one place and 'Tolman *argues*...(present tense)' in another?

3. Check whether subjects and verbs are in agreement. *Everyone* is a singular pronoun. Did you write 'Everyone in *their* (plural) right mind...' when you should have written 'Everyone in her or his right mind...'?

4. Check that sentences are, in fact, sentences, not fragments and not run-ons. If you're using sentence fragments here and there, be certain that they help highlight your points (for example, 'Not likely!') and do not reflect carelessness. Use fragments purposefully, not by accident.

5. Have a trusted friend proofread your papers in exchange for your proofreading the friend's. A page may look correct to you because you are used to looking at it. Errors might leap off the page upon perusal by someone else, however.

6. When in doubt, use the dictionary.

7. Check that your footnotes and references or bibliography contain the information required by your professor and are in the specified format. For most students taking introductory psychology courses, that format will be APA format.

8. Be certain that you have credited your sources so that you are not suspected or accused of plagiarism.

9. At the risk of being boring, I repeat: If the learning center at your college offers a proofreading service, use it.

Proofread to Correct Biased Language The profession of psychology champions the dignity of the individual human being, whether that person is female or male, younger or older, or with or without a psychological disorder.

For example, sexist language is usually biased in favor of males. When talking about a person whose gender is ambiguous, for example, sexist language uses the pronouns *he*, *him*, and *his*. When referring to people or the human species in general, sexist language uses the nouns *man* or *mankind*.

Sexist language also stereotypes people, as in the usage *woman physician* rather than merely *physician*. (The point in the last example is that the writer is suggesting that physicians tend to be men; therefore, the gender must be specified when the physician is a woman.)

The American Psychological Association (1994) also points out many other examples of bias in language. For example, the traditional use of terms such as *subjects*, *receiving treatments*, *schizophrenics*, and *the elderly* denies individuals their dignity and their active participation in research. The APA therefore recommends that we speak of *individuals*, *people*, and *participants*—not of *subjects*. Rathus' textbooks consequently speak of individuals as active in research—as *partaking* in research, or as *obtaining* treatments, not as *receiving* treatments. Rathus' textbooks speak of *people with schizophrenia* or of *people diagnosed with schizophrenia*, not of *schizophrenics*. Rathus' textbooks speak of *older people*, not of *the* elderly. In all of our writings today, the person should always come

Harcourt Brace & Company

first. It is the person that defines the individual. The modifier, whether it refers to age, psychological disorders, or other matters, is secondary. This is not verbal gameplaying. People are people and deserved to be treated with dignity regardless of age, psychological disorder, or participation in research. Our descriptors expand or limit the nature of other human beings, and psychology teaches us that people deserve our consideration.

Table 2 offers examples of biased language and suggestions for correcting it. It is based on the guidelines for reducing biased language as suggested by the American Psychological Association (1994).

Table 2: Examples of Biased Language and How to Correct Them

BIASED USAGE	SUGGESTED ALTERNATIVES
A research subject is required to give *his* informed consent.	A participant in research is required to give informed consent. (*Subject* is changed to *participant*, and *his* is deleted.)
	A participant in research is required to give *his* or *her* informed consent. (*Or her* is added.)
	A participant in research is required to give *her* or *his* informed consent. (Better yet! Varies the traditional practice of putting the man first.)
	Participants in research are required to give *their* informed consent. (Plural form is used.)
	Informed consent is requested from research participants. (Sentence is recast.)
Psychology has advanced our knowledge of *man* (or *mankind*).	Psychology has advanced our knowledge of *human beings* (or *humanity*, or *people*, or *the human species*).
Police*man*, fire*man, mothering,* chair*man*, fresh*man* or fresh*men, girls, Mrs. John Doe*	Police *officer*, fire *fighter, parenting, chair* or chair*person, first-year student(s), women* (unless very young), *Jane Doe*
The study focused on *schizophrenics.*	The study focused on *people diagnosed with schizophrenia.* (People participate in the study, and they should not be stereotyped according to a psychological disorder.)

Continued on next page

Harcourt Brace & Company

BIASED USAGE	SUGGESTED ALTERNATIVES
Control subjects did not *receive* a treatment.	*Individuals in the control group* did not *obtain* the treatment. (The term *subjects* denies people their dignity; it is preferable to speak of *people* or *individuals in a control group.* We can also be more specific; for example, we can say *children in the control group* or *people diagnosed with panic disorder in the control group.* To say that people *receive* a treatment is to portray them as victims and, again, to deny their dignity. It is therefore preferable to say that people *obtain* a treatment, or *participate in* a treatment. We can be more specific here as well; for example, we can say that individuals in the control group *drank* water only, rather than that they *received* water only.)
Blacks are more likely than *whites* to *suffer* from hypertension.	*African Americans* are more likely than *White Americans* to be diagnosed with hypertension. (The American Psychological Association [1994] suggests using the terms *African American* and *White American.* Such terms are not hyphenated, whether they are used as nouns [as in *African Americans*] or adjectives [as in *African American women*]. In other instances, it may be advisable to use the word *Black*, however [as in *Black South Africans* and *White South Africans*].
Oriental people	Use *Asians* (for people in Asia) or *Asian Americans.* Or be more specific, and use *Japanese Americans* or *Chinese Americans.*
The study focused on the problems of *the elderly.*	The study focused on the problems of *older people.*
Homosexuality	Use *a gay male or lesbian sexual orientation.* (The term *homosexuality* is unclear in meaning [that is, does it refer to a sexual orientation or to behavior] and has become connected with stereotyping and prejudice.)
Homosexual behavior	Use *male-male sexual behavior* or *female-female sexual behavior.* (The meaning of *homosexual behavior* is unclear and confuses the concept of sexual orientation with behavior.)
Homosexuals	Use *gay males and lesbians*, or be more specific and use either *gay males* or *lesbians.*

Harcourt Brace & Company

Proofread to Correct Common Errors in Usage Proofread to correct common errors in usage as well. Consider this piece of romantic dialogue:

> 'I love you alot,' said Marsha, 'accept when your mean to me.'
>
> 'Just among you and I,' John responded, 'I'm alright when I'm laying down. You should of known that standing up gives me a headache. Anyways, I didn't no that I had that affect on you.'

All right, I confess: No student of mine ever wrote anything this awful. I had to piece together multiple errors to arrive at this gem.

Table 3 will alert you to a number of common errors in usage. Look for them as you proofread your paper. The table could have been endless; however, I chose to focus on some errors that are likely to make instructors think that students might be better off working in a car wash than taking a course in psychology.

Table 3: Common Errors in English Usage and How to Correct Them

SOURCE OF CONFUSION	CLARIFICATION
Confusing *accept* and *except*	*Accept* is a verb meaning 'to receive favorably' or 'to approve,' as in 'accepting someone's point of view' or 'accepting someone's application to a graduate program in psychology(!)' *Except* can be a verb, meaning 'to leave out,' or a preposition meaning 'leaving out,' as in, 'They invited everyone except me.'
Confusing *advice* and *advise*	*Advice* is a noun, something that is given, as in 'This is my advice to you.' *Advise* is a verb, meaning 'to counsel' or 'to give advice,' as in 'I would advise you to be cautious.'
Confusing *affect* and *effect*	Most of the time, *affect* is a verb meaning 'to stir or move the emotions' or 'to influence.' Consider this example: 'I was affected by the movie.' Most of the time, *effect* is a noun meaning 'something brought about by a cause,' as in the phrase 'cause and effect.' Consider this example: 'The movie had an enormous effect on me.' *Affect* is also used as a noun, but usually only by psychologists and other people who work with individuals who have psychological disorders. In that case, it is pronounced AF-fect and means 'an emotion or emotional response.' *Effect* is also occasionally used as a verb, meaning 'to bring about or produce a result,' as in 'to effect change.'

Continued on next page

Table 3, Continued

SOURCE OF CONFUSION	CLARIFICATION
Confusing *affective* and *effective*	*Affective* is a word usually used only by psychologists or mental-health workers, meaning 'of feelings' or 'of emotions.' Disorders currently referred to as *mood disorders* in the Diagnostic and Statistical Manual (DSM) of the American Psychiatric Association were previously termed *affective disorders*. Unless you are talking about such disorders, you are more likely to be thinking of the word *effective*, meaning 'having an effect' or 'producing results.' Consider this example: 'Lisa made an effective speech.'
Confusing *all right* and *alright*	Use *all right*. *Alright* is technically incorrect, and the Third College (1988) Edition of *Webster's New World Dictionary* (Simon & Schuster) lists 'alright' as a variant spelling of 'all right,' whose usage is disputed. If your instructor marks 'all right' wrong (which sometimes happens!), see him or her during office hours, pull out your dictionary, and be a hero. Be nice, not snide! All right?
Confusing *allot*, *alot*, and *a lot*	Use *a lot* if you mean 'many, plenty' or 'a great deal.' *Allot* (with two *l*'s) is a verb meaning 'to apportion' or 'to distribute.' There is no such word as *alot*. Some instructors may take issue with your ever using *a lot* as well. They may say that '*A lot* is a piece of land' and ask that you use 'much' or 'many' instead.
Confusing *all ready* and *already*	*All ready* means 'Everyone' or 'everything' is 'ready,' as in 'We are all ready to get into the car,' or 'Dinner is all ready.' *Already* means 'done previously,' as in 'I wrote the paper already,' or 'The paper is already finished.' *Already* can also be used at the end of a phrase to express impatience, as in 'Stop it already!' (Or, 'All right, already!' Correctly spelled but ugly, no? [How nice that we agree.])
Confusing *allude*, *elude*, and *illude*	*Allude* means 'to refer,' as in 'I alluded to Skinner's *Walden II* in my paper.' *Elude* means 'to avoid' or 'to escape,' as in, 'He eluded the enemy.' There is no such word as illude.
Confusing *allusion* and *illusion*	An *allusion* is a reference, as in 'I made an allusion to Rogers' *Client-Centered Therapy*.' An *illusion* is 'a false idea or conception,' or 'a misleading appearance.' Consider this example: 'The Ponzo illusion apparently depends on our tendency to assume that the sloping lines are parallel and receding into the distance.'

Continued on next page

Harcourt Brace & Company

Table 3, Continued

SOURCE OF CONFUSION	CLARIFICATION
Confusing *all together* and *altogether*	*All together* means 'all in the same place' or 'all at once,' as in, 'Let's try singing that song again, all together this time.' *Altogether* means 'completely,' as in 'I'm altogether disgusted with the way you did that.'
Confusing *among* and *between*	*Among* is used when there are three or more people or objects. *Between* is usually used when there are two people or objects. 'We had $10 between us' and 'Between you and me' is correct when two people are involved. 'They distributed the money among us' is correct when three or more people have received the money.
Confusing *anymore* with *any more* and *anyplace* with *any place*	Each is always two words. (End of issue.)
Confusing *as* and *like*	As a preposition, *like* means 'similar to' or 'resembling,' as in 'The clouds look like cotton candy,' or 'This problem wasn't like the other problems.' *As* usually means 'to the same degree' ('The missile flew straight as a bullet') or 'at the same time' ('He read as he watched TV').
Confusing *backward* and *backwards*	Use either one! They mean the same thing and are both acceptable. (Enjoy the correctness of both options while you can; you don't have this freedom very often.)
Confusing *bad* and *badly*	*Bad* is an adjective describing states of health and emotions, as in 'He looked bad' and 'She felt bad.' The adverb *badly* describes actions, as in 'He pitched the ball badly.'
Confusing *can* and *may*	*Can* refers to ability or capacity, as in 'Anything you can do I can do better.' *May* refers to permission, as in 'You may not break the law'; and to probability, as in 'That may or may not happen.'
Confusing *cite*, *sight*, and *site*	*Cite* is a verb usually meaning 'to quote' or 'to refer to,' as in, 'She cited the views of many researchers and theorists in her argument.' *Sight* is eyesight, or vision. A *site* is a piece of land, as in the 'site of a work of architecture,' or the place where something happens, as in 'the site of a battle.'
Confusing *complement* and *compliment*	To *compliment* means to praise, whereas to *complement* is to balance or complete.

Continued on next page

Table 3, Continued

SOURCE OF CONFUSION	CLARIFICATION
Confusing *continual* and *continuous*	*Continuous* means without interruption, as in 'The Earth's rotation is continuous.' *Continual* means often, but with interruption, as in 'His continual complaining was quite depressing to his spouse.'
Confusing *credible* and *credulous*	*Credible* means believable, whereas a *credulous* person is gullible, or readily fooled. (Freud might have said that a credulous person was fixated in the oral stage because he would swallow anything.)
Confusing *criteria* and *criterion*	*Criteria* is the plural of *criterion*. You will look very erudite when you use these words correctly in your written work!
Confusing *data* and *datum*	*Data* is a plural noun, and *datum* is singular. A *datum* is a single piece of information, whereas the 'data obtained in a study' usually refers to the entire mass of information assembled. Because *data* is a plural noun, write that 'the data have implications,' not that 'the data has implications.'
Confusing *desert* and *dessert*	The *dessert* is the final course in a meal. *Desert* refers to arid land and, as a verb, means to abandon. E.g., 'He deserted her in the desert, without dessert.' (Hint: remember that *s* stands for 'sweet' and 'dessert' has two s's because it's sweeter. [Ugh.])
Confusing *disinterested* and *uninterested*	*Disinterested* means impartial, unbiased; a judge should be disinterested. *Uninterested* means without interest; a judge should not be *uninterested*.
Confusing *emigrate* and *immigrate*	To *emigrate* is to leave a country; to *immigrate* is to enter a country.
Confusing *eminent* and *imminent*	*Eminent* means respected and well-known, as in 'The eminent psychologist engaged in original research.' *Imminent* means soon to arrive, as in 'imminent disaster.'
Confusing *etc.* and *et al.*	*Etc.* is the abbreviation of *et cetera* and means 'and so forth.' For example, 'The company ran over budget on salaries, paper clips, coffee cups, etc.' *Et al.* is the abbreviation of *et alia*, meaning 'and others.' For most psychology students, use of *et al.* is limited to lists of authors, as in, 'In the study by Saeed et al., it was found that…' Note that the *al.* is followed by a period, whereas *et* is not.

Continued on next page

Harcourt Brace & Company

Table 3, Continued

SOURCE OF CONFUSION	CLARIFICATION
Confusing *farther* and *further*	Today these words appear to be interchangeable, each one meaning 'more distant or remote' or 'additionally.' *Farther* used to be limited in meaning to 'more distant,' however, as in, 'They ran farther,' and *further* used to be limited to 'additionally,' as in 'They further investigated the issue.' You will probably look more sophisticated if you stick to the older usage. You can pull out your dictionary if your instructor takes issue with your usage.
Confusing *few* and *less*	*Few* and *fewer* are used with countable items, as in 'We need fewer people in the room.' *Less* refers to volume or extent, as in 'I need less noise and aggravation.'
Confusing *flammable* and *inflammable*	Despite the fact that the prefix *in-* usually means 'not,' both words have the same meaning: 'capable of catching on fire.'
Confusing *good* and *well*	*Good* is an adjective; *well* is the adverbial form of good. You look *good* [aren't we complimentary?] and you do things *well*. As an adjective, however, *well* means healthy. So 'You look good' means you're attractive, but 'You look well' means you seem healthy.
Confusing *hanged* and *hung*	People are *hanged* [despite one's views on capital punishment] and coats are *hung*.
Confusing *have* and *of*	The confusion here usually occurs in contractions, such as *should've* or *could've*. When you can also use the verb *have*, use *'ve*, not the preposition *of*. Never write could of, should of, would of. (Yes, I know I just wrote them, but I'm the author; I can get away with anything.)
Confusing *I* and *me*	*I* is the subject of a verb, as in 'I am going' or 'She and I are going.' *Me* is the object of a preposition, as in 'Give it to her and (to) me,' or the object of a verb, as in 'Don't discourage John and me.' Write 'He and I gave books to charity,' but write, 'They threw the books at Jack and me.'
Confusing *imply* and *infer*	To *imply* is to suggest, and to *infer* is to deduce or interpret. A literary passage may have *implications*, but readers draw their own *inferences*. Psychologists 'draw inferences' from their data, but the data have implications.

Continued on next page

Table 3, Continued

SOURCE OF CONFUSION	CLARIFICATION
Confusing *important* and *statistically significant*	The words *important* and *significant* are often synonymous. We speak more technically, however, of *statistically significant* differences between group averages or means. In that case, an *important* difference might really matter, but 'important' would not be a technical term. A *statistically significant* difference is a technical term that means unlikely to be due to chance variation.
Confusing *irregardless* and *regardless*	The terms mean exactly the same thing, so use the shorter (more parsimonious?) word, *regardless. Irregardless* is considered nonstandard usage and is technically incorrect.
Confusing *lie* and *lay*	This is where you make your mark! Many well-educated people cringe when they get stuck in a sentence that requires them to choose between the words. The verb *lie* means 'recline,' however, as in 'Lie down' or 'We have to lie low for a while.' (*Lie* also means 'to tell a lie,' of course.) The verb *lay* means 'put or place down' and always takes a direct object, as in 'Lay the book (direct object) on the table.' We also speak of 'laying odds' (placing odds) for a bet, and *lay* is also considered a vulgar term for engaging in sexual activity.

The tenses of *lie* are as follows:

Present tense: *Lie*, as in 'I need to lie down,' or 'We intend to lie in wait right here.'

Past tense: *Lay*, as in 'Earlier this morning I lay down for a while,' or 'This is where they lay in wait the other day.'

Past participle: *Lain*, as in, 'By the time dinner is ready, he had already lain down for a nap,' or 'They had lain in wait for six hours when the sun set.'

The tenses of *lay* are as follows:

Present tense: *Lay*, as in 'Lay down your weapons [objects],' or 'Please lay the foundation [object] for the building.'

Past tense: *Laid*, as in 'They laid down their weapons,' or 'He laid the foundation for the building.'

Continued on next page

Harcourt Brace & Company

Table 3, Continued

SOURCE OF CONFUSION	CLARIFICATION
	Past participle: *Laid*, as in, 'They had already laid down their weapons,' or 'By the time the carpenters were ready, the foundation for te building had been laid.'
	Never, never (never) write or say 'Lay down.' Always use 'Lie down.'
Confusing *leave* and *let*	*Leave* can mean 'to go away'; 'to cause to stay,' as in 'Leave some food'; and 'to bequeath,' as in 'leaving money to one's children or charity.' *Let* usually means 'to allow,' as in 'Let me go' or 'Let it be.' (To *let* an apartment, however, is to rent it.)
Confusing *lend* and *loan*	*Lend* is a verb and *lent* is the past tense, as in 'She lent me some money yesterday.' *Loan* is preferably used as a noun, as in 'She gave me a small loan.' There is no such word as loaned.
Confusing *loose* and *lose*	*Loose* is an adjective, meaning the opposite of tight, as in 'The knot came loose.' *Lose* (pronounced looz) is the verb meaning 'to misplace.'
Confusing *mad* and *angry*	*Mad* means 'insane' in formal usage, not angry. Persons with severe diagnosable psychological disorders might be mad in the sense of having uncontrollable impulses or being delusional. Still, they might be angry if dinner were served late.
Confusing *media* and *medium*	The noun *medium* is singular; *media* is plural. Television is a medium. Television, cinema, and photography are media. The question 'What are the effects of media violence?' means 'What are the effects of violence as shown on TV, in films, etc.?') 'Medium violence,' if you would ever say such a thing, would refer to a moderate amount of violence.
Confusing *ones* and *one's*	*Ones* is a plural noun, as in 'This column contains four ones.' *One's* is possessive, as in 'It is good to do one's own work' (I'm such a moralist). *One's* is also the contraction of one is.
Confusing *phenomena* and *phenomenon*	*Phenomena* is the plural form of *phenomenon*. (Memorize this one along with *criteria* and *criterion*.)

Continued on next page

Harcourt Brace & Company

Table 3, Continued

SOURCE OF CONFUSION	CLARIFICATION
Confusing *principal* and *principle*	A *principal* is an important or central thing or person, as in 'the principal museums of the United States' or the 'principal of the primary school.' A *principle* is a guiding rule, such as the Golden Rule ('Do unto others…').
Confusing *set* and *sit*	To *set* is 'to arrange or put in place.' *Set* takes a direct object, as in 'Set the table [object]' or 'Set the carton [object] down on the floor.' To *sit* is 'to be seated' or 'to remain in place.' *Sit* does not take a direct object, as in 'Please sit down' or 'The vase sits on the mantel.'
Confusing *shall* and *will*	These auxiliary verbs are used to show future tense ('They will be ready tomorrow') or to express determination or obligation ('You shall do what I tell you to do!'). The formal approach of showing the future tense is as follows: I *shall* go tomorrow You (singular) *will* go tomorrow He/she/it *will* go tomorrow We *shall* go tomorrow You (plural) *will* go tomorrow They *will* go tomorrow The formal approach to showing determination or obligation is as follows: I *will* get this done! You (singular) *shall* get this done! He/she/it *shall* get this done! We *will* get this done! You (plural) *shall* get this done! They *shall* get this done! Your instructor may have other ideas. Some instructors–even instructors of English–feel that the formal approach to using these verbs is stuffy or out of touch with the twentieth century. So do not be surprised if you write what is technically correct and are questioned about it. (Bring this book to your instructor during office hours so that I get blamed for it and not you.)

Continued on next page

Harcourt Brace & Company

Table 3, Continued

Source of Confusion	Clarification
Confusing *stationary* and *stationery*	*Stationary* means 'still' or 'in one place,' as in 'In the autokinetic effect, a *stationary* object appears to move.' *Stationery* is what you write on–paper.
Confusing *taught* and *taut*	*Taught* is the past tense of teach. *Taut* means 'tight,' as in 'The rope is taut,' or, metaphorically, 'His nerves were strung taut.'
Confusing *that* and *which*	Clauses that use the relative pronoun *that* are essential to the meaning of a sentence, as in 'The subjects that learned the maze reached the food goal.' Clauses that begin with the relative pronoun *which* add further information but are not essential to the meaning of the sentence, as in 'The subjects, which had an opportunity to explore the maze, were not rewarded for their efforts.'
Confusing *their*, *there*, and *they're*	*Their* is possessive, as in 'They met their obligations.' *There* shows location, as in 'here and there.' *They're* is the contraction of 'they are.'
Confusing *to*, *too*, and *two*	*To* is the preposition that shows location or destination, as in 'Give the book to her' or 'Go to school.' *Too* is the adverb meaning 'also,' as in 'I want to go, too,' or 'extremely,' as in 'That's too much!' *Two* is the number (2).
Confusing *toward* and *towards*	These prepositions have the same meaning and are both considered correct. I recommend using *toward* unless you are quoting someone's speech, in which case you would record what the person said or what you think the person would have said. (*Toward* is consistent with the *Publication Manual's* suggestion that you use economy of expression.)
Confusing *use* and *utilize*	There is a slight difference in meaning between these words; to *utilize* is 'to put to practical or profitable use.' *Utilize* can make it seem that you're trying too hard, and you can't make a mistake if you stick to *use*. In short, use *use* (economy of expression). Don't utilize *utilize*.
Confusing *while* and *although*	*While* is used to connect events that are occurring simultaneously, as in 'Food pellets dropped into the cage while the rat was pressing the lever.'

Continued on next page

Table 3, Continued

SOURCE OF CONFUSION	CLARIFICATION
Confusing *while* and *although* (cont.)	*Although* is used to mean 'whereas' or 'but,' as in 'Although Boyatsis (1974) found that students who drank alcohol behaved more aggressively, Lang (1975) found that students who believed they had drunk alcohol acted more aggressively, whether or not they had actually drunk alcohol.'
Confusing *who* and *whom*	*Who* (or *whoever*) serves as the subject of a verb, as in 'Who did this?!' *Whom* (or *whomever*) serves as the object of a preposition, as in 'To (preposition) whom did you lend my car?' or as the object of a verb, as in 'Choose (verb) whomever you prefer.'
Confusing *whose* and *who's*	*Whose* is possessive, as in 'Whose paper is this? It has no name!' *Who's* is the contraction of 'who has' or 'who is,' as in the bear's lament, 'Who's been sleeping in my bed?'
Confusing *your* and *you're*	*Your* is possessive, as in 'This is your book.' *You're* is the contraction of 'you are,' as in 'I assume that you're going.'

Produce the Final Copy

If you were applying for a job as a management trainee at a bank, would you show up in unwashed jeans and a T-shirt? (Rhetorical question.) Your social psychology chapter indicates that first impressions count. First impressions count with papers, too. I assume that you will want to make a good first impression, to look like a serious contender, to put your best foot forward. You want your paper to look like a serious contender for an A.

Here are some guidelines for producing and packaging the final copy:

1. Consider buying a plastic or paper binder for your paper. Use a binder that's serious and professional looking, not frivolous. Stiff brown paper and clear plastic are superior, for example, to lavender-tinted plastic.

2. Follow the specified format exactly. For most students taking this course, that format will be APA format. Sticking to the format does not guarantee a good grade, but deviating from it will almost certainly hurt your grade.

3. If your professor does not specify a format, ask about her or his preferences.

4. Include a title or cover page (unless instructed not to do so). If your paper is a journal article or is required to look like one, follow the instructions for the title page given on page 5. If, however, you are designing your own title page, I advise including the following information:

   Title of the paper
   Your name
   Title of the course
   Name of your professor
   Date of submission

Harcourt Brace & Company

5. *Spell the professor's name correctly.* You can find the proper spelling in the syllabus, college catalogue, or (usually) on the door of the professor's office.

6. Learn the professor's preferred title (for example, Ms., Dr.) and use it on the title page. A professor who has labored for many years to earn a doctorate may be justifiably annoyed if you do not write 'Dr.' on the title page.

7. If the paper is a term paper, include a table of contents.

8. Use good-quality white paper. Do not use lined paper, onion-skin paper, or the cheapest quality ditto paper.

9. Type your paper, double-spaced. (No excuses!)

10. Back in the days of the Model-T, it used to be said, 'Make my car any color as long as it's black.' Similarly, use any color of ink as long as it's black. (Instructors do not want to be distracted by the color of the ink. A color other than black suggests that you are not a serious student.)

11. Make sure the ribbon is new or nearly new, or that the toner is still black.

12. Use a standard typeface, such as pica or elite, courier or CG Times (point size = 12). Use 10 or 12 characters to the inch. If you're going to be creative, do so in your formation of ideas and in your masterly usage of the English language—not in your typeface. If you're using word processing and a printer, choose a letter-quality (or near-letter-quality) printer, not a dot matrix printer with annoyingly large dots. (Do not cry poverty here until you have done some investigating and learned that your college cannot provide you with access to the printing you need.)

13. Use margins of about an inch all around. Wider margins make a paper look skimpy. Narrower margins make a paper look cramped and hard to read. If you're using computer paper, carefully tear off the edges that contain the guiding holes.

14. Keep a copy of the paper. Professors may decide to hold on to some papers, and now and then a paper gets lost.

HOW TO USE THE EXERCISES IN THIS BOOK

On the following pages are a number of issues and questions addressed in or related to the topics in your introductory psychology textbook. Use principles of critical thinking to analyze each of them. Indicate whether or not you agree with the statements and answer the questions. If you disagree with a statement, as it is written, perhaps you can draft a more carefully thought out, accurate version.

In most cases, I try to get you started by offering some thoughts on how you might critically analyze the issue involved, but feel free to chart your own course, if you prefer. Regardless of whose direction you follow—mine or your own—be skeptical, examine definitions of terms, weigh premises, examine the evidence, and consider whether or not arguments are logical.

You will find extra answer sheets beginning on page 140.

REFERENCES

American Psychological Association. (1994). *Publication manual of the American Psychological Association* (4th ed.). Washington, DC: Author.

Boyer, E. L. (1987). *College: The undergraduate experience in America.* New York: Harper & Row, Publishers.

McGovern, T. (1989). Task force eyes the making of a major. *APA Monitor, 20* (7), 50.

Rathus S. A. (1997) *Essentials of psychology* (5th ed.). Fort Worth: Harcourt Brace College Publishers.

Rathus S. A. (1996) *Psychology in the new millennium* (6th ed.). Fort Worth: Harcourt Brace College Publishers.

Name_____ Date_____

Psychology as a Science—What Is Psychology?

EXERCISE 1: Agree or disagree with the following statement and support your answer: 'Psychology is the scientific study of behavior and mental processes.'

This is probably the most widely used definition of psychology found in introductory psychology textbooks today. It was not always so. Ten to twenty years ago, it was more common to find psychology defined as the scientific study of behavior alone.

What is behavior? What are mental processes? Why do many psychologists insist that the study of mental processes must be included in the definition of the field? What are some of the reasons that other psychologists believe that it is better to exclude mental processes from the definition? What is your view?

Can you arrive at a new definition of psychology that might please everyone?

_____

_____

_____

_____

_____

_____

_____

_____

_____

_____

_____

_____

_____

_____

_____

_____

_____

_____

_____

Harcourt Brace & Company

Name_____ Date_____

Psychology as a Science—Science and Human Behavior

EXERCISE 2: Agree or disagree with the following statement and support your answer:
'It is possible to understand human behavior from a scientific perspective.'

Can the richness and complexity of human behavior be reduced to scientific statements? What is human behavior? What is science?

Which, if any, aspects of human behavior seem subject to scientific analysis?

_____

_____

_____

_____

_____

_____

_____

_____

_____

_____

_____

_____

_____

_____

_____

_____

_____

_____

_____

_____

_____

_____

_____

Harcourt Brace & Company

Name_____   Date_____

Psychology as a Science—History and Diversity

EXERCISE 3: Psychology's 'top ten,' as selected both by historians of psychology and chairpersons of psychology departments, consists completely of white males. Why do you think that is this so?

_____

Table 1 ranks the top ten ('most important') historic figures in psychology according to a recent survey of historians of psychology and chairpersons of psychology departments (Korn et al., 1991). The historians and chairpersons concur on seven of the 'golden oldies.'

What are the possible explanations for the list's consisting of only white men? Is it conceivable that only white males have made key contributions to psychology? What are some of the contributions that have been made by women and people of color?

TABLE 1
Historians' and Chairpersons' Rankings
of the Importance of Figures in the History of Psychology

	HISTORIANS			CHAIRPERSONS	
Rank	Figure	Area of Contribution	Rank	Figure	Area of Contribution
1.	Wilhelm Wundt	Structuralism	1.	B. F. Skinner	Operant Conditioning
2.	William James	Functionalism	2.	Sigmund Freud	Psychoanalysis
3.	Sigmund Freud	Psychoanalysis	3.	William James	Functionalism
4.	John B. Watson	Behaviorism	4.	Jean Piaget	Cognitive Development
5.	Ivan Pavlov	Conditioning	5.	G. Stanley Hall	Development
6.	Hermann Ebbinghaus	Memory	6.	Wilhelm Wundt	Structuralism
7.	Jean Piaget	Cognitive Development	7.	Carl Rogers	Self Theory, Person-Centered Therapy
8.	B. F. Skinner	Operant Conditioning	8.	John B. Watson	Behaviorism
9.	Alfred Binet	Assessment of Intelligence	9.	Ivan Pavlov	Conditioning
10.	Gustav Theodor Fechner	Psychophysics	10.	Edward L. Thorndike	Learning—Law of Effect

Rankings are based on data from Korn, J. H., Davis, R., R., & Davis, S. F. (1991). Historians' and chairpersons' judgments of eminence among psychologists. *American Psychologist, 46*, 789–792.
Harcourt Brace & Company

Name_____ Date_____

EXERCISE 3, continued:

Harcourt Brace & Company

Psychology as a Science

EXERCISE 4: Do students really need to take course work in psychology to understand other people? After all, as one student put it, 'I've been observing people for my whole life.'

Since students have observed other people for many years before entering this course, many are tempted to believe that they are already 'psychologists.' How scientific are their observations likely to be, however? What sources of error or bias are found in people's everyday observations of other people? How do the methods of observation used by psychologists attempt to control for such errors and biases?

_____

_____

_____

_____

_____

_____

_____

_____

_____

_____

_____

_____

_____

_____

_____

_____

_____

_____

_____

_____

Psychology as a Science—Correlation Versus Cause and Effect

EXERCISE 5: Does alcohol cause aggression?

Alcohol is clearly connected with, or linked to, aggression. Many crimes of violence are committed by people who have been drinking. What does the word 'cause' mean, however?

What is the preferred psychological research method for showing cause and effect? (What kind of research can you devise in an effort to answer this crucial question?)

_____

_____

_____

_____

_____

_____

_____

_____

_____

_____

_____

_____

_____

_____

_____

_____

_____

_____

_____

_____

_____

Name_____   Date_____

Psychology as a Science—Research with Lower Animals

EXERCISE 6: Agree or disagree with the following statement and support your answer:
'Research with lower animals cannot really tell us anything about people.'

What kinds of things can animal research tell us about people? What kinds of things can be learned only by using human subjects in research? Why? (In arriving at an answer, you may wish to distinguish between behavior and mental processes, and to consider the different areas of research undertaken by psychologists–biopsychology, sensation and perception, motivation and emotion, personality, social psychology, and so on.)

_____

_____

_____

_____

_____

_____

_____

_____

_____

_____

_____

_____

_____

_____

_____

_____

_____

_____

_____

_____

_____

Psychology as a Science—Ethics

EXERCISE 7: Is it ethical to deceive human subjects as to the nature of psychological research?

Consider some studies that could not have been carried out without deceiving human subjects as to their purposes and methods. Is it ethical to deceive subjects as to the purposes and methods of the research? What is meant by the principle of informed consent? Is deception of subjects consistent or inconsistent with this principle?

In your response, try to consider the value of some of the studies in which subjects have been deceived. Is it possible to weigh or balance the value of the research findings against the harm—or potential harm—done by the use of deception?

_____

_____

_____

_____

_____

_____

_____

_____

_____

_____

_____

_____

_____

_____

_____

_____

_____

_____

_____

_____

Harcourt Brace & Company

Biology and Behavior—Why Do Psychologists Study Biology?

EXERCISE 8: Since psychology is usually defined as the study of behavior and mental processes, why are psychologists interested in biological matters such as the nervous system, the endocrine system, and heredity?

Can knowledge of the brain and other parts of the nervous system enhance our understanding of behavior and mental processes? If so, how? What are the connections between the endocrine system and emotional experience?

Do any behavior patterns and mental abilities seem linked to heredity? What kinds of behaviors? (Which psychoanalyst believed that people inherit thoughts that date to prehistory?)

_____

_____

_____

_____

_____

_____

_____

_____

_____

_____

_____

_____

_____

_____

_____

_____

_____

_____

_____

_____

Biology and Behavior–Psychology and Religion

EXERCISE 9: What do the discoveries about the biological basis for thinking and feeling suggest about the theological concept of the soul?

Do these biopsychological discoveries scientifically invalidate the concept of the soul? Do these discoveries reveal how God used neurons, neurotransmitters, and so on in the creation of the soul? Do the concepts of 'mind,' 'cognition,' and 'soul' overlap, or are they separate and distinct from one another? What do you think?

_____

_____

_____

_____

_____

_____

_____

_____

_____

_____

_____

_____

_____

_____

_____

_____

_____

_____

_____

_____

Biology and Behavior–The Nervous System

EXERCISE 10: Agree or disagree with the following statement and support your answer: 'The mind is a function of the brain.'

What is meant by the 'mind'? Can the   exist without the brain?
functions that people attribute to 'the mind'

_____

_____

_____

_____

_____

_____

_____

_____

_____

_____

_____

_____

_____

_____

_____

_____

_____

_____

_____

_____

Name_____ Date_____

Biology and Behavior–The Nervous System

EXERCISE 11: Agree or disagree with the following statement and support your answer:
'Some people are left-brained, and other people are right-brained.'

What would it mean for a person to be 'left-brained' or 'right-brained'? Is evidence concerning the functioning of the hemispheres of the brain fully consistent with this notion?

_____

_____

_____

_____

_____

_____

_____

_____

_____

_____

_____

_____

_____

_____

_____

_____

_____

_____

_____

_____

_____

_____

Harcourt Brace & Company

Name_____   Date_____

Biology and Behavior–The Nervous System

EXERCISE 12: Although split-brain surgery severs the brain in two, is it truly possible for people to have two brains? What would it be like if you had two such brains?

What is the brain? What does it mean to have a split brain? What does research show about people who have such operations? Would it be possible to have different thoughts or personalities in each 'brain'? Is there any connection between split-brain research and multiple personality?

_____

_____

_____

_____

_____

_____

_____

_____

_____

_____

_____

_____

_____

_____

_____

_____

_____

_____

_____

Name_____ Date_____

Biology and Behavior–The Nervous System

EXERCISE 13: If psychologists discovered a pleasure center in people's brains that were as powerful and rewarding as the pleasure centers in the brains of rats, would people, like rats, do whatever they could to stimulate these centers until they dropped from exhaustion?

What do you think is the role of pleasure in determining or guiding human behavior? Are people's motives basically biological–built into the brain or other parts of the body? Do you seem to be guided or pushed by cognitive or spiritual motives? Might you be fooling yourself? What do you think? Why?

_____
_____
_____
_____
_____
_____
_____
_____
_____
_____
_____
_____
_____
_____
_____
_____
_____
_____
_____
_____

Harcourt Brace & Company

Biology and Behavior–Heredity

EXERCISE 14: Agree or disagree with the following statement and support your answer:
'Since psychological traits such as introversion, intelligence, and aggressiveness are influenced by heredity, there is no point to trying to encourage the introverted to be more sociable, to helping poor students do better in school, or to teaching aggressive people other ways of getting what they want.'

What does psychological evidence suggest about the roles (and limits) of the influences of heredity and environmental influences on human behavior? What is meant by the *interaction* of nature and nurture?

_____

_____

_____

_____

_____

_____

_____

_____

_____

_____

_____

_____

_____

_____

_____

_____

_____

_____

Name_____ Date_____

Sensation and Perception–Signal Detection

EXERCISE 15: Do we sometimes fail to hear things because we don't want to hear them?

What is the relationship between sensation and perception? What are the effects of motivation on perception? What insights are offered by signal-detection theory?

_____

_____

_____

_____

_____

_____

_____

_____

_____

_____

_____

_____

_____

_____

_____

_____

_____

_____

_____

_____

_____

_____

Harcourt Brace & Company

Name_____ Date_____

Sensation and Perception–Sensory Adaptation

EXERCISE 16: Because of sensory adaptation, we become less sensitive to our familiar surroundings. Does this loss of sensitivity deprive us of useful information (and of the ability to enjoy constant pleasures!), or does it help us pay attention to what is most important?

Does sensory adaptation help us filter the sensory wheat from the chaff? Can these questions be answered with simple yes's or no's?

_____

_____

_____

_____

_____

_____

_____

_____

_____

_____

_____

_____

_____

_____

_____

_____

_____

_____

_____

_____

Sensation and Perception

EXERCISE **17**: Visually normal people have feature detectors for lines that are presented at various angles, and they can also see the colors of the visible spectrum. What could our sensory worlds be like if we had feature detectors for other visual stimuli, or if we could see lights at much higher and lower frequencies? What if our senses of smell were as powerful as those of dogs, or if we could hear sounds as high in frequency as dogs do?

Here is a flight of fancy! Would you like to get philosophical and speculate on whether or not people can sense the information that is most crucial for them to be aware of? Might there be a thing as too much sensory stimulation, or would sensory adaptation come to the rescue? What do you think?

_____

_____

_____

_____

_____

_____

_____

_____

_____

_____

_____

_____

_____

_____

_____

_____

_____

_____

_____

_____

_____

Harcourt Brace & Company

Sensation and Perception–Vision

EXERCISE 18: You and another person may agree that a piece of fruit is red or green. You may both answer 'Orange' when you are placed in separate rooms and separately asked the color of the same sheet of paper. Can you know what the other person is seeing, however? Can you assume that the other person sees the same thing in his or her 'mind's eye'?

It is a simple matter to devise experiments to determine whether or not you and other people will independently agree as to what color objects are. (Isn't it?) Do these same experiments indicate what you and the other person are imagining or picturing in your minds when you say 'orange' or 'blue' or 'red,' however? If not, can you think of a research approach that could answer such questions?

_____

_____

_____

_____

_____

_____

_____

_____

_____

_____

_____

_____

_____

_____

_____

_____

_____

_____

Sensation and Perception

EXERCISE **19**: What are the implications of knowledge of the biological aspects of sensation and perception for helping people with sensory disabilities? How might powerful computers and complex electrical circuits be used to help blind people to see, deaf people to hear?

Allow yourself to develop fanciful notions that assume the existence of more powerful computers than we have today, and of microscopic electric circuits that are not yet available. (These notions may not be all that far-fetched!)

_____

_____

_____

_____

_____

_____

_____

_____

_____

_____

_____

_____

_____

_____

_____

_____

_____

_____

_____

_____

_____

Harcourt Brace & Company

Name_____   Date_____

Sensation and Perception–Pain

EXERCISE 20: Agree or disagree with the following statement and support your answer:
'The best way to cope with pain is to ignore it.'

_____

What types of things happen within the body when we are assaulted by painful stimuli? How do our attitudes toward pain exacerbate or limit pain? What are some of the ways in which psychologists help people cope with pain? Do psychological methods for coping with pain differ from medical methods for doing so? If so, how?

_____

_____

_____

_____

_____

_____

_____

_____

_____

_____

_____

_____

_____

_____

_____

_____

_____

_____

_____

Sensation and Perception–Extrasensory Perception

EXERCISE **21**: Agree or disagree with the following statement and support your answer:
'Some people have the ability to read other people's minds.'

What does it mean to 'read another person's mind'? How might our answers to this question differ, depending on how one defines 'mind reading'? Might the statement, for example, be interpreted to mean that some people can accurately predict other people's behavior on the basis of their body language and their behavior in similar past situations? How would this interpretation yield a different answer from one that interpreted mind reading as directly perceiving the thoughts of another person?

_____

_____

_____

_____

_____

_____

_____

_____

_____

_____

_____

_____

_____

_____

_____

_____

_____

_____

_____

                                            Harcourt Brace & Company

Name_____ Date_____

Consciousness

EXERCISE 22: Can we understand or study the consciousness of another person?

What is consciousness? Can we directly observe another person's consciousness, or is consciousness a 'private' matter? How do we arrive at conclusions concerning other people's thought processes? What are the limitations of our methods?

In your answer, you may wish to consider areas of psychology that would seem to address issues related to consciousness—for example, sensation and perception, problem-solving, intelligence, creativity, and attitude formation and change. What methods do psychologists use in these areas? Do these methods appear to assess consciousness? If so, how?

_____

_____

_____

_____

_____

_____

_____

_____

_____

_____

_____

_____

_____

_____

_____

_____

_____

_____

Sleep

EXERCISE 23: How much sleep do you need?

Can you be certain how much sleep you need? How do you arrive at your estimate? How do you evaluate the adequacy of your personal 'research'?

_____

_____

_____

_____

_____

_____

_____

_____

_____

_____

_____

_____

_____

_____

_____

_____

_____

_____

_____

_____

_____

Dreams

EXERCISE 24: Agree or disagree with the following statement and support your answer:
'People can gain insight into their inmost feelings and fears by interpreting their dreams.'

What theory of dreams is being referred to in this statement? What is meant or suggested by the words *insight* and *inmost*? What is meant by an interpretation of a dream? What is the evidence for the idea that the content of dreams might represent deep-seated feelings such as fears?

How often do you dream? What kinds of dreams do you have? Are your dreams filled with mythical kingdoms and monsters or with the humdrum events of the day? Do you have nightmares? Do nightmares seem to come at particular times or at random? Do your dreams seem to serve any purpose for you? Does your 'interpretation' of your dreams today differ from the view of dreams you had prior to taking this course? If so, how?

_____

_____

_____

_____

_____

_____

_____

_____

_____

_____

_____

_____

_____

_____

_____

_____

_____

Name_____ Date_____

Effects of Alcohol

EXERCISE 25: Agree or disagree with the following statement and support your answer: 'People cannot be held responsible for their behavior when they have been drinking.'

What are the effects of alcohol on cognition and behavior? What does 'responsibility' mean? What kinds of behaviors are being referred to in this item? What are the roles alcohol itself and of drinkers' expectations about the effects of alcohol in influencing the behavior of drinkers? (Hint: Even if someone were to regularly lose control over his or her behavior when drinking, would not he or she be responsible for choosing to drink?)

You may also consider this issue from another angle: What would be the social implications of accepting the statement as written?

_____

_____

_____

_____

_____

_____

_____

_____

_____

_____

_____

_____

_____

_____

_____

_____

_____

_____

Harcourt Brace & Company

Effects of Alcohol

EXERCISE 26: Agree or disagree with the following statement and support your answer:
'Some people just can't hold their liquor.'

What does it mean–to 'hold' one's liquor? Does it refer to the concept of *tolerance*? If so, what factors appear to be connected with tolerance for alcohol? Which factor or factors are genetic or inborn, and which appear to be experiential? (What does the word *just* imply in such a statement.)

_____

_____

_____

_____

_____

_____

_____

_____

_____

_____

_____

_____

_____

_____

_____

_____

_____

_____

_____

_____

Substance Use and Abuse

EXERCISE 27: Agree or disagree with the following statement and support your answer:
'Cocaine and narcotics such as heroin are the most dangerous psychoactive drugs.'

Note the use of the word *psychoactive* in the statement; cocaine and narcotics are only being compared to other drugs that might be used to alter consciousness or, perhaps, induce feelings of euphoria or relaxation–*not* to poisons such as curare. Nevertheless, your answer is likely to depend on which drugs you think of (don't forget alcohol and nicotine!) and on your definition of the word *dangerous*.

As you think about this issue, will you use *dangerous* to mean physically dangerous ounce for ounce? Will you use *dangerous* to mean detrimental to the health of the user, to society at large? Will you be thinking in terms, say, of one overdose, or will you be thinking in terms of the total cost to society of the drugs in question? Should you, for example, be considering fatal, alcohol-related auto accidents?

_____

_____

_____

_____

_____

_____

_____

_____

_____

_____

_____

_____

_____

_____

_____

_____

Name_____   Date_____

Meditation

EXERCISE 28: Agree or disagree with the following statement and support your answer:
'Through meditation, people have been able to transcend the boundaries of everyday experience.'

The statement, as written, may be suggestive of many kinds of spiritual or special experience. In your answer, however, define or delimit terms such as *transcend* and *everyday experience*. The nature of your answer, and the strength of your arguments, will surely depend on the definitions you use. If you do wish to delve into transcendental experiences in the sense of spiritual experiences, it will probably be advisable to discuss the nature and limits of the kinds of psychological research that can address such issues. The concept of *transcending everyday experience* can also be understood—much more mundanely, of course!–in terms of doing things that enable us to surmount daily anxieties and tensions.

_____

_____

_____

_____

_____

_____

_____

_____

_____

_____

_____

_____

_____

_____

_____

_____

_____

Biofeedback Training

EXERCISE 29: Agree or disagree with the following statement and support your answer:
'Research into biofeedback training has altered the traditional distinction between *voluntary* and *involuntary* body functions.'

What *is* the traditional distinction between voluntary and involuntary body functions? (You may wish to refer to various branches or divisions of the nervous system, such as the autonomic nervous system, as you contemplate your answer.) Definitions are important is contemplating this issue. For example, you can raise your heart rate by running around a track. If you choose to raise your heart rate by doing so, can you be said to be *voluntarily* raising your heart rate? Or, within the science of psychology, does *voluntary* behavior refer in more limited fashion to directly willed behavior? If so, does research show that people given biofeedback training can learn to directly will their hearts to accelerate or decelerate?

_____

_____

_____

_____

_____

_____

_____

_____

_____

_____

_____

_____

_____

_____

_____

_____

_____

_____

_____

_____

Name_____   Date_____

Hypnotism

EXERCISE 30: A friend claims to have been finally 'cured' of smoking by a hypnotist. Can hypnotism cause people to stop smoking?

What does your textbook suggest that hypnotism is? Does hypnotism control the behavior of people? Why would a smoker seek the help of a hypnotist? Why might a person stop smoking after visiting a hypnotist? Here is a related question that may help you focus in on your answer: Which of the following two people is more likely to be helped to stop smoking by a hypnotist–the one who believes in hypnotism or the one who does not? Why?

_____

_____

_____

_____

_____

_____

_____

_____

_____

_____

_____

_____

_____

_____

_____

_____

_____

Learning–What Is Learning?

EXERCISE **31**: How shall we define *learning*? Is learning a relatively permanent change in behavior that arises from experience? Is learning a process by which experience contributes to relatively permanent changes in the way organisms mentally represent the environment? Can you think of a superior definition?

The first definition is behavioral. Learning is defined in terms of the measurable events or changes in behavior by which it is known. The second definition is cognitive. From the cognitive perspective, learning is *made evident* by behavioral change, but learning is defined as an internal and not directly observable process.

What are the implications of these contrasting definitions for understanding behavior and mental processes? Which of them, to you, seems closer to the mark? Why? Can you arrive at a third and superior definition? Can you create a definition that will satisfy cognitive and behavioral psychologists? (If so, get ready to receive your Nobel prize.)

_____

_____

_____

_____

_____

_____

_____

_____

_____

_____

_____

_____

_____

_____

     Harcourt Brace & Company

Name_____   Date_____

Learning–Learning Versus Instinct

EXERCISE 32: In human beings, what kinds of behavior patterns are learned and what kind are innate (inborn)? Are most differences between people learned or innate?

What do we mean by 'differences' between people? Food preferences, religious or political differences, or sexual interests? Differences in language or intelligence? If we focus on language or intelligence, we may want to refer to the textbook's discussions of these issues. Also, what does the second question mean by 'most' differences? Do we require more precise (more scientific) language?

_____

_____

_____

_____

_____

_____

_____

_____

_____

_____

_____

_____

_____

_____

_____

_____

_____

_____

_____

_____

_____

Name_____   Date_____

Learning–Importance of Pleasure and Pain

EXERCISE 33: Agree or disagree with the following statement and support your answer: 'Human behavior is under the governance of pleasure and pain.'

Some philosophers (for example, Hobbes, Descartes, and Bentham) argued that people are basically motivated to try to achieve pleasure and avoid pain. Some psychologists (for example, Thorndike and Hull) bring this notion into learning theory through the concepts of rewards and punishments. To what extent is human behavior learned mechanically by means of rewards and punishments? How do we explain people's choices to do painful things (for example, sacrifice themselves for others) or to forego pleasures (for example, deny themselves desserts or immoral sexual liaisons)?

_____

_____

_____

_____

_____

_____

_____

_____

_____

_____

_____

_____

_____

_____

_____

_____

_____

_____

Harcourt Brace & Company

Learning–Conditioning and Complex Behavior

EXERCISE 34: Agree or disagree with the following statement and support your answer: 'Apparently complex human behavior can be explained as the summation of so many instances of conditioning.'

This item invites you to consider the complexity and richness of human behavior qualitatively and quantitatively. If you see the complexity and richness of human behavior as basically similar to that of lower animals, you may tend to agree with the statement. If you see human behavior as essentially different from that of lower animals, such as flatworms (*planaria*), you may be more likely to disagree with the statement.

Does human behavior appear to involve cognitive maps, insights, and self-direction? If so, can these features be explained in terms of the summation of so many instances of conditioning?

_____

_____

_____

_____

_____

_____

_____

_____

_____

_____

_____

_____

_____

_____

_____

_____

_____

_____

Learning–Learning and Motor Skills

EXERCISE 35: Pianists' fingers 'fly' over the keys faster than they can read notes or even think notes. What kinds of learnings are at work in learning to play the piano, or in learning to perfectly execute a piece with rapid notes?

Piano playing (and music appreciation) are certainly examples of behaviors (and mental processes) that differentiate people from lower organisms. Is there, however, a role for simpler learnings–for conditioning–in explaining the ability to play the piano and other instruments? Can the playing of one note come to serve as the stimulus for playing the second? Is there a role for cognitive learning? (For example, for deciding to learn to play the piece? For planning to practice? For deciding on a method of attack?)

Harcourt Brace & Company

Learning–Latent Learning

EXERCISE 36: Agree or disagree with the following statement and support your answer:
'E. C. Tolman's research in latent learning disproves principles of conditioning.'

Tolman's classic research in latent learning appears to challenge principles of operant conditioning. It suggests that animals learn in the absence of reinforcement and form cognitive maps (mental representations) of their environments. Is it possible to explain the results of Tolman's research more mechanistically? Is it possible, for example, that animals such as laboratory rats mechanically acquire drives to learn about their environments because such learnings may eventually be reinforced? Is it possible, too, that a cognitive map is nothing more than the summation of a great numbers of learned responses to a great number of stimuli that involve sensory-motor coordination? Is there something compelling about research in latent learning (or about research into insight learning) that suggests that cognitive learning differs in quality from conditioning? What do you think?

If you believe that latent learning cannot be explained in terms of principles of conditioning, might there nevertheless be a role for conditioning in explaining behavior?

_____

_____

_____

_____

_____

_____

_____

_____

_____

_____

_____

_____

_____

_____

_____

_____

_____

Name_____ Date_____

Learning–Effects of Media Violence

EXERCISE 37: Does violence on television and in films cause aggression in viewers?

Is there a connection between media violence and aggressive behavior in viewers? Is the connection correlational or causal? What is a *correlation*? What is a *cause* of behavior? How do we define aggression? What is the nature of the psychological evidence on the matter?

What of the 'selection factor'? What kinds of audiences are drawn to films such as *Colors*, *Boyz N the Hood*, and *Juice*?

_____

_____

_____

_____

_____

_____

_____

_____

_____

_____

_____

_____

_____

_____

_____

_____

_____

_____

_____

_____

_____

Harcourt Brace & Company

Memory–Procedural Memory

EXERCISE 38: Agree or disagree with the following statement and support your answer:
'You never forget how to ride a bicycle.'

What kinds of learning and memory are involved in bicycle riding? Does the statement show insight into the formation and retention of certain kinds of memories, yet, perhaps, go too far in its assertion that one **never** forgets how to ride a bicycle? What types of evidence may one draw upon in supporting or disconfirming this statement? What do you think?

_____

_____

_____

_____

_____

_____

_____

_____

_____

_____

_____

_____

_____

_____

_____

_____

_____

_____

_____

_____

_____

_____

Memory–Models of Memory

EXERCISE 39: Agree or disagree with the following statement and support your answer: 'The memory is like a muscle. The more we practice using it, the better it becomes.'

How meaningful is it to compare memory to a muscle? What does 'practicing' memory mean? If the statement is interpreted as referring to rote repetition, is there evidence that learning by rote facilitates future learning by rote? If the statement refers to mnemonic devices, is the use of such devices analogous to flexing and strengthening muscles?

Harcourt Brace & Company

Memory–Reconstructive Memory

EXERCISE 40: Agree or disagree with the following statement and support your answer:
'People's memories are distorted by their attitudes and stereotypes.'

This statement addresses the issue as to whether memories are clear snapshots or colored by our *schemas* (ways of filtering or interpreting experience), some of which may be prejudices and stereotypes. The statement also seems to suggest that we may sometimes remember things the way we want to remember them. Put it another way: are memories pure impressions of the stimuli that we observe or are they reconstructed on the basis of these stimuli and personal biases?

What does memory research such as that by Elizabeth Loftus and her colleagues suggest about the roles of schemas in recalling information?

_____

_____

_____

_____

_____

_____

_____

_____

_____

_____

_____

_____

_____

_____

_____

_____

Memory–Permanence of Long-Term Memories

EXERCISE 41: Agree or disagree with the following statement and support your answer:
'People never forget their experiences–regardless of whether or not they can summon them to mind upon request.'

What theoretical ideas underlie the notions that people never forget their experiences? How does the statement relate to psychodynamic theory, Wilder Penfield's biological ideas, and to theories concerning organization in long-term memory? For example, is it possible that you remember something but cannot bring it to conscious awareness because you lack the proper retrieval cues? Or because other learning interfered with its retrieval? Is it possible to *disprove* the idea that you 'remember' everything but may not be able to bring certain things to awareness because of the lack of cues?

_____

_____

_____

_____

_____

_____

_____

_____

_____

_____

_____

_____

_____

_____

_____

_____

_____

Harcourt Brace & Company

Memory–Rote Rehearsal

EXERCISE 42: Agree or disagree with the following statement and support your answer:
'The best way to remember information to repeat it over and over again.'

The statement refers to rote repetition, which is one form of rehearsal of information. Is rote repetition the best way to remember information? All kinds of information? If rote repetition is not always the best way to remember information, what kinds of information may be best learned by rote repetition, and which may not be?

_____

_____

_____

_____

_____

_____

_____

_____

_____

_____

_____

_____

_____

_____

_____

_____

_____

_____

_____

Memory–Flashbulb Memories

EXERCISE 43: How is it that some event make such an impression on us that we never forget them, whereas many or most events are lost in the wake of time?

This question can refer to those memories referred to as 'flashbulb memories' and to others. What are flashbulb memories? How do theorists explain the retention of flashbulb memories? What is suggested by William James's comments:

Memory requires more than mere dating of a fact in the past. It must be dated in my past. In other words, I must think that I directly experienced its occurrence. It must have that 'warmth and intimacy'...as characterizing all experiences 'appropriated' by the thinker as his own.

_____

_____

_____

_____

_____

_____

_____

_____

_____

_____

_____

_____

_____

_____

_____

_____

_____

_____

_____

Harcourt Brace & Company

Name_____   Date_____

Language–Which Species Use Language?

EXERCISE **44**: Agree or disagree with the following statement and support your answer:
'Only human beings can really use language.'

What does the word 'really' mean in this statement? (Would other words have been more appropriate?) What is meant by 'language'? What does the definition of language suggest about whether or not the waggles of bees or the chirps of birds are instances of language? What does the evidence suggest about whether or not the signing of apes is *real* use of language?

_____

_____

_____

_____

_____

_____

_____

_____

_____

_____

_____

_____

_____

_____

_____

_____

_____

_____

_____

Name_____   Date_____

Language–Language Acquisition

EXERCISE 45: Agree or disagree with the following statement and support your answer: 'People acquire language on the basis of experience.'

Critical thinkers avoid overgeneralizations. Is experience necessary for language learning? Sure. A child (or adult) who has never heard English will not be able to understand Shakespeare (or any English speaker). But is exposure to language a *sufficient* factor in language learning? (Have you ever taught your cocker spaniel to speak?–not to bark on command, but to really speak a language!)

Consider the evidence presented in your textbook for various theories of language acquisition as you go about responding to this statement.

_____

_____

_____

_____

_____

_____

_____

_____

_____

_____

_____

_____

_____

_____

_____

_____

_____

_____

_____

Harcourt Brace & Company

Name_____ Date_____

Intelligence–Intelligence and Achievement

EXERCISE 46: Agree or disagree with the following statement and support your answer:
'Some children are overachievers in school.'

What does the statement mean? What is *achievement*? What is *overachievement*? Overachievement relative to *what*?

People who might concur with this statement probably read it to mean that some children do better in school than one might expect on the basis of the intelligence. What is the connection between achievement and intelligence? What does it mean if a child exhibits an average performance on an intelligence test but his or her schoolwork is consistently good to excellent? In your discussion, you may wish to differentiate between the concepts of intelligence and IQ. You may also wish to refer to concepts such as the reliability and validity of intelligence tests.

_____

_____

_____

_____

_____

_____

_____

_____

_____

_____

_____

_____

_____

_____

_____

_____

Intelligence–Individual and Cultural Differences

EXERCISE 47: Are there real social-class, racial, and ethnic differences in intelligence?

Consider operational definitions. What is meant by a *real* difference? (Is a 'real' difference a genetic difference? A large difference? A statistically significant difference?) What is meant by the term *intelligence*?

What does the evidence show about racial and social-class differences in intelligence test scores, or IQs? Do these IQs represent intelligence? Or do they represent *real* intelligence? Why or why not?

This question, as you can see, was not worded in a scientifically accurate manner. It nevertheless addresses an issue that interests millions of people–and affects billions!–and is thus worthy of your consideration. In your answer, you may therefore try to 'translate' it into more scientific language and then answer it on the basis of evidence.

_____

_____

_____

_____

_____

_____

_____

_____

_____

_____

_____

_____

_____

_____

_____

_____

_____

_____

Harcourt Brace & Company

Intelligence–Cultural Bias in Testing

EXERCISE 48: Agree or disagree with the following statement and support your answer:
'It is not possible to construct a truly culture-free intelligence test.'

Are there are culture-free or culture-fair intelligence tests? What does psychological evidence reveal about the performance of white, middle-class children and of minority children on such tests?

What types of cultural influences or biases affect people's performances on intelligence tests? Does cultural influence or bias refer only to the kinds of information to which people are exposed, or does it also refer to culturally-influenced motivation to perform well on tests and to adjustment to the test-taking situation?

_____

_____

_____

_____

_____

_____

_____

_____

_____

_____

_____

_____

_____

_____

_____

_____

_____

_____

_____

_____

Intelligence–Head Start

EXERCISE 49: Agree or disagree with the following statement and support your answer:
'The effects of Head-Start programs are illusory. You can't really boost children's IQs.'

Here again we have that pudding-like word, 'really.' The simple answer to this question would seem to be, 'Sure you can!' What is an 'IQ,' however? Is it an assumed inborn psychobiological characteristic, or a score on an intelligence test? (The latter is scientifically accurate, of course.)

The question, as phrased, oversimplifies the issue. Let us thus recast the question into something more meaningful, such as 'Is it possible to really boost children's learning ability or just their performance on a test?' Now, to what kind of research does this question refer?

Harcourt Brace & Company

Name_____   Date_____

Motivation–Is There a Maternal Instinct in Humans?

EXERCISE 50: Agree or disagree with the following statement and support your answer: 'Women make natural mothers.'

A trick question? Not really. What do you think is suggested by the phrase 'natural mother'? Are we talking about becoming the biological mother of a child or about knowledge and use of expert child-rearing practices? If we are talking about the latter, the issue becomes whether or not women have 'natural instincts' that induce them to want children and to love children, and that show them how to rear children.

Motivation–Sensory Deprivation

EXERCISE 51: Agree or disagree with the following statement and support your answer:
'Some people may find a long, relaxing vacation on the beach to be highly annoying.'

No doubt about it–many people claim to have just such a response to what most people might expect to be a relaxing experience. What does psychological research suggest about the types of individual differences that might account for this reaction to basking in the sun?

_____

_____

_____

_____

_____

_____

_____

_____

_____

_____

_____

_____

_____

_____

_____

_____

_____

_____

_____

_____

Harcourt Brace & Company

Name_____   Date_____

Psychology

EXERCISE 52: Why do some people seem satisfied to just get by, whereas other people are driven to work and improve despite their achievements?

This question would seem to refer to more than one area of psychological research. It touches upon issues related to the need for achievement, the Type-A behavior pattern, and, perhaps, genetic differences and differences in child-rearing practices.

Emotion–Lie Detection

EXERCISE **53**: What do lie detectors detect?

What are 'lie detectors'? (What is the more scientific name for such instruments?) What can we *demonstrate* that lie detectors measure?

What are the relationships between the body responses measured by lie detectors and lying? What does the evidence suggest?

_____

_____

_____

_____

_____

_____

_____

_____

_____

_____

_____

_____

_____

_____

_____

_____

_____

_____

_____

_____

_____

   Harcourt Brace & Company

Emotion–Theories of Emotion

EXERCISE 54: Which is more basic to our emotional reactions to events–our physiological arousal (body responses) or our cognitive evaluations of events?

Consider these lines by poet e. e. cummings:

> *since feeling is first*
> *who pays any attention*
> *to the syntax of things*
> *will never wholly kiss you . . .*
> **–e. e. cummings**

There are many theories of how and why we react emotionally. The cummings poem suggests that our bodies, including then reactions of our autonomic nervous systems, react first to events. Some psychologists might agree that we respond more or less automatically to events. Other psychologists argue that our cognitive appraisals of events influence our feelings and our body responses.

What are emotions? What are the relationships between body responses, such as those of the autonomic nervous system, cognitive appraisals, and emotions? What does the evidence suggest? What do you think?

_____

_____

_____

_____

_____

_____

_____

_____

_____

_____

_____

_____

_____

_____

_____

_____

_____

_____

Name_____   Date_____

Emotion–Love

EXERCISE 55: Can love last, or is it but a passing fancy?

As a critical thinker, you will want to focus on definitions. What does *love* mean here? Does the question refer to romantic love, the kind of love that parents and children feel toward one another, or to the kind of love that is shared by lifetime companions?

Which kind of love is most likely to be a passing fancy? What does psychological research suggest about the abiding nature of various kinds of love?

_____

_____

_____

_____

_____

_____

_____

_____

_____

_____

_____

_____

_____

_____

_____

_____

_____

_____

_____

Harcourt Brace & Company

Motivation–Hunger

EXERCISE 56: Agree or disagree with the following statement and support your answer:
'Dieting is the normal way of eating for American women.'

Critical thinkers are precise in their definitions of terms and recognize that the accuracy of arguments depends on the meanings of the words that are used.

What are some ways of defining the word 'normal'? One has to do with statistical normality; from this perspective, if many or most people do it, it's normal. Another has to do with notions as to what is proper or ideal. People selecting this sort of definition might have a different response to the them.

_____

_____

_____

_____

_____

_____

_____

_____

_____

_____

_____

_____

_____

_____

_____

_____

_____

_____

_____

_____

_____

_____

Motivation–Hunger

EXERCISE 57: Agree or disagree with the following statement and support your answer:
'People who are overweight simply eat too much.'

This statement reflects a widely held view that the overweight cannot or–perhaps more to the point–will not control what they eat and therefore eat too much. The statement, like many other kinds of common sense (or common nonsense) overgeneralizes and has a moralistic tint.

Critical thinkers avoid overgeneralizations, however. What kinds of factors are shown by psychological research to be involved in obesity? Do **all** of them involve eating too much? (What, by the way, does 'too much' mean?) Do some people, for example, find it difficult to lose weight even when they consume fewer calories than weight charts recommend to maintain their weights?

_____

_____

_____

_____

_____

_____

_____

_____

_____

_____

_____

_____

_____

_____

_____

_____

_____

_____

Name_____   Date_____

Developmental Psychology–Surrogate Motherhood

EXERCISE **58**: Who is the baby's real mother–the surrogate mother or the wife of the man who fathers the baby?

When a hired surrogate mother is artificially inseminated by the husband of an infertile women, and agrees to surrender the baby at birth, who is the real mother? The mother who conceived and carried the baby in the uterus, or the wife of the father? What is a 'real mother'? Is motherhood basically a biological or psychosocial concept? Is surrogate motherhood the mirror image of artificial insemination?

_____

_____

_____

_____

_____

_____

_____

_____

_____

_____

_____

_____

_____

_____

_____

_____

_____

_____

_____

_____

Developmental Psychology—Nature–Nurture Controversy

EXERCISE 59: Agree or disagree with the following statement and support your answer: 'Human development is self-regulated by the unfolding of natural plans and processes.'

This statement is clearly consistent with the maturationist views of Arnold Gesell and other psychologists who have leaned heavily toward genetic (as opposed to environmental) explanations of the processes of development. You may wish to critically examine this statement by questioning whether it is an overgeneralization. Does it apply equally, that is, to all areas of development? Does it apply equally, for example, to physical development, perceptual development, cognitive development, personality development, and social development?

Many contemporary psychologists also believe that such statements oversimplify the processes of development and that development represents the *interaction* of nature and nurture. What do you think?

_____

_____

_____

_____

_____

_____

_____

_____

_____

_____

_____

_____

_____

_____

_____

_____

_____

_____

Developmental Psychology–Prenatal Development and Abortion

EXERCISE 60: Agree or disagree with the following statement and support your answer:
'Abortion is the taking of a human life.'

Abortion is a controversial and divisive topic. The statement 'Abortion is the taking of a human life' arouses powerful passions (pro and con), but it is also subject to critical analysis. In evaluating the statement, begin by defining terms. For example, what does the phrase 'human life' mean? There would be universal (or nearly universal) agreement that a sperm cell and an unfertilized egg cell do not constitute human life–although they are both made up of living tissue. There would also be nearly universal agreement that newborn babies do constitute human life. The conflict involves the period between conception and birth.

Psychological knowledge of prenatal development cannot exactly define when 'human life' begins, but it may suggest more refined questions. For example, is a zygote (a fertilized egg cell) a human life? If not, why not? If so, in what way? Does human life begin when the dividing mass of cells becomes implanted in the uterine wall? Does it begin when the major body organ systems (such as the nervous system) have been formed? When the heart begins to beat? When the fetus starts to look like a person? (When does that happen?) When the fetus is 'viable' or capable of 'independent life'? What is meant by 'independent life'?

Although the science of psychology does not reveal when human life begins, critical thinking that is based on psychological knowledge may help you refine your own views.

More than 1.5 million abortions are performed in the United States each year. Abortion is practiced widely in Canada, Japan, Russia, and many European nations. Abortion is rarely used as a primary means of birth control. It usually comes into play when other methods have failed.

The national debate over abortion has been played out in recent years against a backdrop of demonstrations, marches, and occasional acts of violence, such as fire-bombings of abortion clinics. Many members of the Right-to-Life (pro-life) movement assert that human life begins at conception and thus views abortion as the murder of an unborn child. Many in the pro-life movement brook no exception to their opposition to abortion. Some would permit abortion to save the mother's life, however, or when a pregnancy results from rape or incest.

The pro-choice movement contends that abortion is a matter of personal choice and that the government has no right to interfere with a woman's right to terminate a pregnancy. Pro-life advocates argue that women should be free to control what happens within their bodies, including the right to terminate a pregnancy.

Moral concerns about abortion often turn on the question of when human life begins. In his thesis on *ensoulment*, the thirteenth-century Christian theologian St. Thomas Aquinas wrote that a male fetus does not acquire a human soul until 40 days after conception, and a female fetus, 90 days. Neither the Old nor New Testaments specifically prohibit abortion, but for much of its history, the Roman Catholic Church held to St. Thomas Aquinas's belief that ensoulment of the fetus with a human soul did not occur for at least 40 days after conception. In 1869, Pope Pius IX declared that human life begins at conception. Abortion at any stage of pregnancy thus became murder in the eyes of the church and grounds for excommunication. The Roman Catholic Church has since remained staunchly opposed to abortion during any stage of pregnancy.

Scientists, too, have attempted to define when human life can be said to begin. Astronomer Carl Sagan, for example, writes that fetal brain activity can be considered a secular or scientific marker of human life. Brain activity is needed for human thought, the quality that is considered most 'human' by many. Brain wave patterns typical of children do not begin until about the thirtieth week of pregnancy. Before then, the human fetus lacks the brain architecture to begin thinking. Of course, the question is raised as to whether we can equate fetal brain wave activity with human thought. (What would a fetus think about?) Moreover, some argue that a newly fertilized ovum carries the *potential* for human thought in the same way that the embryonic or fetal brain does. It could even be argued that sperm cells and ova are living things in that they carry out the biological processes characteristic of cellular life. All in all, the question of when *human* life begins may be a matter of definition that is unanswerable by science.

_____

_____

_____

_____

_____

_____

_____

_____

_____

_____

_____

_____

_____

_____

_____

_____

_____

_____

_____

_____

_____

_____

_____

Name_____ Date_____

Developmental Psychology–Cognitive-Developmental Theory

EXERCISE **61**: Agree or disagree with the following statement and support your answer:
'Children are natural scientists who actively intend to learn about and manipulate their worlds.'

The view of children as actively intending to learn about and manipulate the environment is one of the key concepts of cognitive-developmental theory. The behaviorist view, by contrast, is that people essentially react to environmental stimuli rather than intending to interpret and act on the world. If people at time seem to be acting intentionally, it is because they are shaped to do so.

Which view–cognitive-developmental or behaviorist–is more consistent with your own? Which view do you like better? Why? Does evidence concerning the behavior of children (and adults) seem more supportive of one view than the other? What do you think?

_____

_____

_____

_____

_____

_____

_____

_____

_____

_____

_____

_____

_____

_____

_____

_____

_____

_____

_____

_____

Developmental Psychology–Adolescence

EXERCISE **62**: G. Stanley Hall wrote that adolescence is a period of *Sturm und Drang*–storm and stress. Is it? If so, why?

Hall attributed the conflicts and distress of adolescence to biological changes, in which case we might expect typical adolescent behavior patterns, such as mood swings. Is the evidence overall suggestive of the dominance of biological factors during adolescence, or do cultural influences and social expectations also play key roles?

_____

_____

_____

_____

_____

_____

_____

_____

_____

_____

_____

_____

_____

_____

_____

_____

_____

_____

_____

_____

Harcourt Brace & Company

Developmental Psychology–Child Abuse

EXERCISE 63: Are child abusers likely to have been victims of abuse themselves?

What does research say about the relationships between victimization as a child and subsequent abuse of one's own children? Is the notion that child abusers were victimized themselves oversimplified?

_____

_____

_____

_____

_____

_____

_____

_____

_____

_____

_____

_____

_____

_____

_____

_____

_____

_____

_____

_____

_____

Name_____ Date_____

Personality–Psychodynamic Theory

EXERCISE 64: Do unconscious impulses and ideas influence our behavior?

What does the term 'unconscious' mean?   What is the nature of the evidence for psychodynamic theory?

_____

_____

_____

_____

_____

_____

_____

_____

_____

_____

_____

_____

_____

_____

_____

_____

_____

_____

_____

_____

_____

_____

Harcourt Brace & Company

Name_____   Date_____

Personality–Psychodynamic Theory

EXERCISE 65: Agree or disagree with the following statement and support your answer:
'People are basically antisocial. Their primitive impulses must be suppressed and repressed if they are to function productively within social settings.'

What theory of personality is suggested by this statement? Is the statement capable of proof or disproof? Can you devise an experiment that would answer the question? What theoretical, practical, and ethical considerations might prevent us from running such an experiment?

_____

_____

_____

_____

_____

_____

_____

_____

_____

_____

_____

_____

_____

_____

_____

_____

_____

_____

_____

_____

Name_____   Date_____

Personality–Personality and Gender

EXERCISE 66: Agree or disagree with the following statement and support your answer:
'A woman's place is in the home.'

Who decides about 'a woman's place'—women or men? What theoretical views and social forces may have given birth to the view that a woman's place is in the home? Does psychology have anything to contribute to the debate over 'a woman's place'?

_____

_____

_____

_____

_____

_____

_____

_____

_____

_____

_____

_____

_____

_____

_____

_____

_____

_____

_____

_____

_____

                                   Harcourt Brace & Company

Personality–Humanistic—Existential Theory

EXERCISE 67: Agree or disagree with the following statement and support your answer:
'People are basically prosocial. They only engage in antisocial behavior when their natural prosocial tendencies have been thwarted.'

What theory of personality is suggested by this statement? Is the statement capable of proof or disproof? Can you devise an experiment that would answer the question? What theoretical, practical, and ethical considerations might prevent us from running such an experiment?

_____

_____

_____

_____

_____

_____

_____

_____

_____

_____

_____

_____

_____

_____

_____

_____

_____

_____

_____

_____

_____

_____

Personality–Personality and Stability of Behavior

EXERCISE 68: Agree or disagree with the following statement and support your answer: 'People don't really change.'

This statement is overly general. People clearly *do* change in many ways. They mature, they learn new languages and skills, and, in my case, they lose their hair. What, then, are people who make such statements usually referring to? I have heard the comment many times in reference to the benefits (or lack of benefits) of psychotherapy. The point to the statement is that the personality, to paraphrase William James, is set in plaster by a certain age. To what theory or theories of personality might such a statement refer?

To support or contest the statement, why not try delimiting it to more specific notions related to personality. Also consider the meaning of the word *really*. That is, what does it mean for a person to *really change* as opposed to simply *change*? Perhaps a *real* change would be a change in personality, as opposed to a change in *behavior*? Perhaps the personality change might seem more real because the person's behavior would then change across many different situations? Would not behaviorists counter that we can only make inferences about personality from behavior? My thinking is done. It's your turn.

_____

_____

_____

_____

_____

_____

_____

_____

_____

_____

_____

_____

_____

_____

_____

Harcourt Brace & Company

Personality–Learning Perspectives and Personal Freedom

EXERCISE 69: Given cultural and social conditioning, is true freedom possible? Is freedom merely an illusion?

You have freedom when you're easy in your harness.
    –Robert Frost

The views of John B. Watson and B. F. Skinner largely discard the notions of personal freedom, choice, and self-direction. Most of us assume that our wants originate within us. But Skinner suggests that environmental influences such as parental approval and social custom shape us into *wanting* certain things and *not wanting* others. To Watson and Skinner, even our telling ourselves that we have free will is determined by the environment as surely as is our becoming startled at a sudden noise.

What is *freedom*? What is *true* freedom? (Does 'true freedom' differ from 'freedom' or does the phrase simply overdescribe the concept?) Is it possible that people can be shaped into telling themselves (believing) that they are free when their behavior is actually quite circumscribed within social and cultural limits? Is it possible, for example, that people in the United States are compelled to see themselves as being free to choose their own attitudes and behaviors? If so, would it be possible to see through such cultural conditioning?

Name_____   Date_____

Personality–Social-Learning Theory

EXERCISE 70: Agree or disagree with the following statement and support your answer:
'Success breeds success.'

_____

Does success breed success? Are people who believe that they can succeed more likely to succeed?

What is the connection between a 'success experience' and self-confidence? What is the connection between self-confidence (positive self-efficacy expectancies) and performance?

_____

_____

_____

_____

_____

_____

_____

_____

_____

_____

_____

_____

_____

_____

_____

_____

_____

_____

Harcourt Brace & Company

Personality–Tests and Measurements

EXERCISE 71: Can people create whatever impression they wish to create on personality tests?

Does it depend on the test to some degree? Can they guess what responses to the Rorschach or TAT might mean? Can they misrepresent on the MMPI without also getting revealing scores on the test's validity scales?

_____

_____

_____

_____

_____

_____

_____

_____

_____

_____

_____

_____

_____

_____

_____

_____

_____

_____

_____

_____

Health Psychology–Psychological Factors in Physical Illness

EXERCISE 72: What are the connections between psychological factors such as attitudes and physical illnesses? How can psychological variables affect physical health?

When Norman Cousins, former editor of the *Saturday Review*, was hospitalized for a rare and painful illness, he was a 'bad' patient. He complained about hospital routines such as the low-calorie and tasteless diet, the indiscriminate taking of x-rays, and the heavy administration of drugs including pain-killers and tranquilizers. Even with all these procedures, his doctors gave him only a slim chance of a full recovery.

As he related in his book, *Anatomy of an Illness*, Cousins decided to take things into his own hands. First, he moved from the hospital setting–which encourages passive compliance with the patient role–to a hotel room. Second, he traded the massive doses of analgesics and other drugs for laughter and vitamins. He watched films of the Marx Brothers and of his favorite TV comedy shows and focused on maintaining a positive attitude. To his physicians' amazement, he made a substantial recovery from his illness.

What does Cousins' experience suggest about the connections between attitudes and illness? Does research tend to support or contradict the wisdom of Cousins' behavior?

Harcourt Brace & Company

Health Psychology–Predictability as a Moderator of Stress

EXERCISE 73: Agree or disagree with the following statement and support your answer: 'It is better not to know about bad things that are going to happen.'

To know or not to know–that is the question

Have you heard the old saw that you're better off not knowing certain things, or better off not knowing too much? How can this cliché be connected to research concerning the effects of predictability of stressors as moderators of their impact? Could the statement be partly true, or true for some people? Is it possible that some people are better off 'knowing,' whereas others are not? What does the research suggest?

_____

_____

_____

_____

_____

_____

_____

_____

_____

_____

_____

_____

_____

_____

_____

_____

_____

_____

_____

_____

Health Psychology–Health Locus of Control

EXERCISE **74**: Agree or disagree with the following statement and support your answer:
'Good health is basically a matter of heredity or good luck. People cannot really do much to enhance their health or stave off illness.'

Many people assume that whether or not they become ill or remain healthy is the luck of the draw. Consider the phrase 'being *struck* by illness.' It implies that illness comes out of the blue. There are, of course, many different kinds of illnesses, from 'garden variety' flu and upset stomach to cancer and heart disease. Today, however, it seems that the public has become more aware that behavior can have an effect on the probability of contracting *some* illnesses. In thinking critically about this issue, try to weigh the evidence to arrive at some more useful hypotheses about behavior and health. For example, are there relationships between stressors, attitudes, behavior patterns, and illness? What are they?

_____

_____

_____

_____

_____

_____

_____

_____

_____

_____

_____

_____

_____

_____

_____

_____

_____

_____

    Harcourt Brace & Company

Health Psychology–Coronary-Prone Personality

EXERCISE **75**: Is there such a thing as a coronary-prone personality?

You may have heard that it is unwise to 'work oneself up into a heart attack.' (Who can argue?) The question, of course, is whether any particular personality dispositions or behavior patterns are in fact connected with the risk of heart disease. What does the evidence suggest, for example, about the possible role of Type-A behavior?

_____

_____

_____

_____

_____

_____

_____

_____

_____

_____

_____

_____

_____

_____

_____

_____

_____

_____

_____

Health Psychology–Cancer-Prone Personality

EXERCISE 76: Is there such as thing as a cancer-prone personality?

Are people with certain psychological traits or dispositions more likely to contract cancer? What does the research suggest? Can you explain why certain traits, such as prolonged depression, may affect the risk of cancer?

_____

_____

_____

_____

_____

_____

_____

_____

_____

_____

_____

_____

_____

_____

_____

_____

_____

_____

_____

_____

_____

                                    Harcourt Brace & Company

Abnormal Psychology–Normalcy and the Cultural Context

EXERCISE 77: Agree or disagree with the following statement and support your answer: 'Normalcy and abnormality must be understood within a particular cultural context.'

Are there some behaviors that might be considered normal in one culture but abnormal within another? (What model of abnormal behavior suggests that abnormal behaviors are *caused* by sociocultural factors such as poverty and discrimination?) Are there behaviors that would be considered abnormal in every culture? What kinds of behaviors?

What of what we called the 'generation gap' when I was a graduate student? Are there behavior patterns or customs that seem quite normal to you but impress your parents or your grandparents as abnormal or as deviant?

_____

_____

_____

_____

_____

_____

_____

_____

_____

_____

_____

_____

_____

_____

_____

_____

_____

_____

Abnormal Psychology–Normalcy of Anxiety and Depression

EXERCISE **78**: Agree or disagree with the following statement and support your answer:
'People should not feel anxious or depressed.'

The Constitution of the United States provides us with the rights to 'life, liberty, and the pursuit of happiness.' It sometimes seems that Americans are required to be happy, in fact. Feelings of anxiety and depression seem to be equated with abnormality. Statistically speaking, however, most of us feel anxious or depressed from time to time. In thinking critically about this issue, what criteria are usually used in determining whether or not behavior or feelings are abnormal?

My feeling is that the statement 'People should not feel anxious or depressed' is oversimplified and overgeneralized. Can you explain why?

_____
_____
_____
_____
_____
_____
_____
_____
_____
_____
_____
_____
_____
_____
_____
_____
_____
_____
_____

Name_____   Date_____

Abnormal Psychology–Responsibility for Behavior

EXERCISE 79: Agree or disagree with the following statement and support your answer: 'Mentally ill people cannot be held responsible for their behavior.'

In thinking critically about this issue, you may want to consider the controversy generated by the insanity plea. John Hinckley, for example, was found not guilty of attempting to assassinate President Reagan by reason of insanity.

You may also wish to define some terms: What is meant by 'mentally ill'? What is meant by 'responsible'? What is meant by 'behavior'? Is the term *behavior* limited to criminal behavior, or does it extend to avoidance behavior, as in a phobic individual's avoidance of fear-inducing stimuli? In the case of Hinckley, the issue might be translated into the following: 'Schizophrenic people cannot be held responsible for attempted murder.' In the case of a phobic individual, the issue might be translated as, 'People with phobias for hypodermic syringes cannot be held responsible for avoiding injections.'

Critical thinkers do not overgeneralize. Is the statement more accurate for people with some psychological disorders than for people with others?

_____

_____

_____

_____

_____

_____

_____

_____

_____

_____

_____

_____

_____

_____

_____

_____

Abnormal Psychology–Schizophrenia

EXERCISE 80: Agree or disagree with the following statement and support your answer: 'Schizophrenia runs in families and is therefore caused by genetic factors.'

Yes, schizophrenia does run in families. It's what follows the 'therefore' that creates the controversy in this statement. Let me give you a few related questions to consider in your response: Are traits or problems that run in families necessarily genetic? If one can inherit a predisposition toward schizophrenia, does the predisposition guarantee that one will exhibit the disorder? What other factors may be involved?

_____

_____

_____

_____

_____

_____

_____

_____

_____

_____

_____

_____

_____

_____

_____

_____

_____

_____

_____

_____

_____

_____

Harcourt Brace & Company

Abnormal Psychology–Suicide

EXERCISE 81: Agree or disagree with the following statement and support your answer:
'You have to be insane to want to take your own life.'

People have a tendency to label behavior that they do not like or understand as 'sick' or 'insane.' According to *Webster's New World Dictionary*, insanity is 'not a technical term' in psychology. In law, insanity is a mental condition 'that makes a person incapable of what is regarded legally as normal, rational conduct or judgment.' In critically thinking about this issue, consider the information about suicide presented in your introductory psychology textbook and pay attention to the definition of insanity.

Let's suggest that you avoid *circular reasoning*. It would be circular reasoning to say, for example, that 'Suicide is proof of insanity' and then to use this 'premise' to show that a person who killed herself or himself was insane.

Methods of Therapy–Psychotherapy Versus Common Sense

EXERCISE 82: Agree or disagree with the following statement and support your answer: 'Psychotherapy is just common sense.'

This belief is perhaps a corollary of the view that everyone and anyone is a psychologist on the basis of life experiences. On the basis of life experiences, cannot anyone offer advice to the troubled?

As a psychologist I would disagree with this statement. I would define *psychotherapy* and talk about the kinds of knowledge and training that shape psychologists into therapists.

What do you think? Why?

_____

_____

_____

_____

_____

_____

_____

_____

_____

_____

_____

_____

_____

_____

_____

_____

_____

_____

Name_____   Date_____

Methods of Therapy–Psychoanalysis

EXERCISE 83: Agree or disagree with the following statement and support your answer:
'The effects of traditional psychoanalysis cannot be determined by the experimental method.'

Although psychoanalytically oriented treatment methods fare reasonably well in therapy-outcome studies, many psychoanalysts argue that traditional psychoanalysis cannot be subjected to experimental analysis.

Does this claim make sense or not? In arriving at your own conclusions, consider experimental research methods, including the functions of random assignment, control groups, and 'blinds.' Also consider the methods of traditional psychoanalysis.

_____

_____

_____

_____

_____

_____

_____

_____

_____

_____

_____

_____

_____

_____

_____

_____

_____

_____

Methods of Therapy–Behavior Therapy

EXERCISE 84: Is behavior therapy behavioral?

This is not a trick question. Consider some of the principles of behaviorism, as described in your introductory psychology textbook. Then consider definitions and of behavior therapy and various behavior-therapy techniques. You will find that behavior therapists use many methods such as systematic desensitization and modeling that involve mental imagery and learning by observation. So is behavior therapy behavioral? Does much depend on how behavior therapy is defined? Would such methods cause behavior therapy to be disowned by behaviorists like John B. Watson and B. F. Skinner?

_____

_____

_____

_____

_____

_____

_____

_____

_____

_____

_____

_____

_____

_____

_____

_____

_____

_____

    Harcourt Brace & Company

Methods of Therapy–Assessment of Efficacy of Psychotherapy

EXERCISE 85: Justin swears he feels much better because of psychoanalysis. Deborah swears by her experience with Gestalt therapy. Are these endorsements acceptable as scientific evidence? Why or why not?

Most of us know people who endorse certain kinds of psychotherapy, or megavitamins, or even spiritual healing. In critically thinking about the endorsements of Justin and Deborah, consider the ways in which their experiences fall short of the kinds of research methods that psychologists find to be acceptable. For example, were they randomly assigned to their therapies? Were there control groups? Were efforts made to control for their expectations? How is 'feeling much better' operationally defined and measured?

_____
_____
_____
_____
_____
_____
_____
_____
_____
_____
_____
_____
_____
_____
_____
_____
_____
_____
_____

Methods of Therapy–Assessment of Efficacy of Psychotherapy

EXERCISE 86: Agree or disagree with the following statement and support your answer:
'It has never been shown that psychotherapy does any good.'

This statement may be at best outdated. (At worst, it is prejudiced and just plain foolish.) Perhaps it reflects a reaction to the types of anecdotes reported by Justin and Deborah (see Exercise 85). It is also consistent with the views expressed in a paper published by Hans Eysenck in 1952. Eysenck argued that although most people who had psychotherapy showed improve-ment, it had not been shown that the effects of psychotherapy were superior to 'spontaneous remission'–getting better, that is, simply as a function of the passage of time.

What is the current status of the evidence concerning the effects of psychotherapy? Is it still possible to maintain that the effects of psychotherapy are not superior to spontaneous remission? Does the statement overgeneralize? Is it possible, that is, to lump all forms of psychotherapy together?

_____

_____

_____

_____

_____

_____

_____

_____

_____

_____

_____

_____

_____

_____

_____

Methods of Therapy–Chemotherapy

EXERCISE 87: Agree or disagree with the following statement and support your answer:
'Drugs cause more problems than they solve when they are used to treat people with abnormal behavior problems.'

Drugs is a buzz word, a loaded term (consider the 'Just say no' to drugs campaign). Drugs as a method of therapy are known more technically as chemotherapy, however, and their use is discussed in your textbook's chapter on methods of therapy.

In thinking critically about this statement, try to avoid overgeneralizing. Is chemotherapy, for example, of greater benefit with some problems than with others?

_____

_____

_____

_____

_____

_____

_____

_____

_____

_____

_____

_____

_____

_____

_____

_____

_____

_____

_____

_____

Gender–Gender Differences

EXERCISE 88: Agree or disagree with the following statement and support your answer:
'Men are more aggressive than women.'

Is the answer obvious? Look before you leap.

Men usually (but not always) behave more aggressively than women. Is behaving more aggressively than women the equivalent of *being* more aggressive than women, however? Are men biologically predisposed toward being more aggressive than women? What does the evidence suggest? Is cultural conditioning the central reason that men behave more aggressively? What of situational factors? What kinds of circumstances narrow the 'aggression gap' between women and men?

_____

_____

_____

_____

_____

_____

_____

_____

_____

_____

_____

_____

_____

_____

_____

_____

_____

_____

_____

Harcourt Brace & Company

Homosexuality

EXERCISE 89: Agree or disagree with the following statement and support your answer: 'Homosexuality is a sexual preference.'

Critical thinking involves careful examination of the meanings and implications of words. How does the concept of 'sexual preference' differ from that of 'sexual orientation'? Is heterosexuality a sexual preference or an orientation? (If you are a heterosexual, how much **choice** do you perceive yourself to have?)

Date Rape

EXERCISE 90: Agree or disagree with the following statement and support your answer:
'A woman who is raped is partly to blame if she agrees to go to the man's room or home.'

Note the premises implicit in this statement. One is that sexual relations between women and men are an adversarial contest. Another is that women who act seductively or who agree to go 'part way' are teases if they refuse to engage in sexual intercourse.

How do statements such as these help create a social climate that contributes to the likelihood of rape?

_____

_____

_____

_____

_____

_____

_____

_____

_____

_____

_____

_____

_____

_____

_____

_____

_____

_____

    Harcourt Brace & Company

Name_____   Date_____

H.I.V. Infection and AIDS

EXERCISE 91: Agree or disagree with the following statement and support your answer:
'One's behavior, and not one's group membership, places one at risk of H.I.V. infection.'

What is meant by group membership? How do people in various groups become infected by H.I.V.? Can you become infected if you do not belong to a high-risk group?

_____

_____

_____

_____

_____

_____

_____

_____

_____

_____

_____

_____

_____

_____

_____

_____

_____

_____

_____

_____

H.I.V. Infection and AIDS

EXERCISE 92: Agree or disagree with the following statement and support your answer:
'Safe sex is the answer to the AIDS epidemic.'

'Safe sex' is certainly being touted as a proper approach to many young people. There are many aspects of this statement to consider, however, and doing so will enhance you critical thinking.

What, for example, is meant by 'the answer to the AIDS epidemic'? What will 'safe sex' do for people who are already infected with H.I.V.? What of the role of values? Should public authorities be promoting safe sex in general, or presenting safe sex as an avenue for dealing with the AIDS epidemic by people who are sexually active and intend to have multiple partners? How safe is 'safe sex,' moreover? What kinds of behavior patterns are included under the heading 'safe sex'? Are they all safe? Are they equally safe?

The statement 'Safe sex is the answer to the AIDS epidemic' may be at best a well-intentioned overgeneralization.

_____

_____

_____

_____

_____

_____

_____

_____

_____

_____

_____

_____

_____

_____

_____

Social Psychology–Attitudes and Behavior

EXERCISE 93: Agree or disagree with the following statement and support your answer: 'People vote their consciences.'

The statement sounds right and assumes that we can predict people's behavior from knowledge of their attitudes. On the other hand, how many people actually vote? Moreover, can we always predict people's behavior from knowledge of their expressed attitudes? Even if we know of people's genuine attitudes, is their behavior always consistent with their attitudes?

_____

_____

_____

_____

_____

_____

_____

_____

_____

_____

_____

_____

_____

_____

_____

_____

_____

_____

_____

_____

Social Psychology–Persuasion and Advertising Claims

EXERCISE 94: Agree or disagree with the following statement and support your answer:
'Our product is superior to Brand X.'

Ah, that infamous Brand X! In considering advertising claims, first write in a product that is advertised extensively in the media: _____. Then record some of the advertising techniques: For example, who endorses the product? What claims are made about the product?

1. _____

2. _____

3. _____

Now critically evaluate this advertising campaign on the basis of your knowledge of techniques that are used to persuade people to change their attitudes and behaviors.

_____

_____

_____

_____

_____

_____

_____

_____

_____

_____

_____

_____

_____

_____

_____

Social Psychology–Cognitive Dissonance

EXERCISE 95: Given the power of attitude-discrepant behavior and of social influences, how can any of us know where social and cultural influences end, and our real selves begin?

Psychology and American ideals of freedom both focus on the dignity and behavior of the individual, but is it truly possible for us to become our 'real selves,' or 'our own persons'? As illustrated by the case of Patty Hearst, social psychology raises the question as to whether or not we can determine where our own selves begin and the influences of others–family members, religious leaders, media personalities, and so on–leave off. In thinking critically about this issue, can you operationally define the concept of a 'real self'? Can you devise research that might answer the question?

The real-life kidnapping of newspaper heiress Patty Hearst provides a case study of the ways in which attitude-discrepant behavior might be able to change our concepts of who we are and what we stand for.

Patty was an undergraduate student at Berkeley in the 1970s, when she was abducted by a radical group (the 'SLA'). Early messages from the SLA directed the Hearst family to distribute millions of dollars' worth of food to the poor if they wished their daughter to live. There was no suggestion that Patty was a willing prisoner.

A couple of months later, SLA communiqués contained statements by Patty that she had willingly joined them. Patty declared her revolutionary name to be Tania and sent a photograph in which she wore a guerrilla outfit and held a machine gun. She expressed contempt for her parents' capitalist values and referred to them as pigs. Patty and other SLA members then robbed a San Francisco bank. Patty was videotaped brandishing a rifle. She was reported to have threatened a guard. Patty later fired an automatic rifle to cover other SLA members as they fled from a store they had robbed.

When Patty was captured by the FBI, she was defiant at first. She gave a revolutionary salute and identified herself as Tania. Once she was in prison, her identity appeared to undergo another transformation. She asked to be called Patty again. At her trial she seemed remorseful. The defense argued that had it not been for the social influence of the SLA, Patty would never have engaged in criminal behavior or adopted revolutionary values.

How is it that a college undergraduate with typical American values came to express attitudes that were opposed to her lifelong ideals? How is it that other people, when they come under the influence of 'Moonies' or other cults show conversion in some of their most basic attitudes and behavior patterns?

Can Patty's conversion in self-identity can be explained through cognitive-dissonance theory? After Patty's kidnapping, she was exposed to fear and fatigue and forced into attitude-discrepant behavior. She was coerced into expressing agreement with SLA values, engaging in sexual activity with SLA members, and training for revolutionary activity. As long as she clung firmly to her self-identity as Patty, these repugnant acts created cognitive dissonance. By adopting the suggested revolutionary identity of Tania, however, Patty could look upon herself as 'liberated' rather than as a frightened captive or as a criminal. Not only was her fear of her captors reduced. Her cognitive dissonance was reduced as well because her behavior was not inconsistent with her newly adopted values.

Which was the *real* Patty? The college student or the radical? Does the answer depend on who Patty is with at the time? Are our self-identities also malleable and shapeable by the people with whom we live or work or play? How can we know?

(Write your answer on the following page.)

Social Psychology–Interpersonal Attraction

EXERCISE 96: Agree or disagree with the following statement and support your answer: 'Opposites attract.'

Here is a 'truism.' Are not women and men opposites, and are they not attracted to one another? (Watch out–Don't be too quick to grant me my premise that women and men are 'opposites.' Are they?) Are we not drawn to 'forbidden fruit'? Of course, if we limit our definition of 'opposites' to people of the opposite gender, we'll be on safe ground when we claim that 'Opposites attract'–at least most of the time. Will our conclusions be the same when we critically examine this maxim on the basis of having opposing attitudes?

Name_____   Date_____

Social Psychology–Social Influence

EXERCISE 97: Agree or disagree with the following statement and support your answer:
'The Nazis who participated in the slaughter of European Jews were a particularly evil and abnormal group of people.'

How, many psychologists have wondered, could the Nazis engage in such horrible crimes? Were they psychopaths? Were they psychotic? Were they possessed by evil? One of the most chilling possibilities is that many Nazis were normal people (we cannot speak for all of them) who were functioning in a social system in which brutal murder was the norm, and that most of them were trying to impress their bosses just like 'workers' in many other kinds of 'jobs' try to impress their bosses.

What does psychological research in the area of social influence suggest about the ability of the 'average' citizen to participate in great crimes? (You may go beyond the basic requirements of this question by looking into research on Nazis. What did psychologists who interviewed and tested Nazis discover?)

_____

_____

_____

_____

_____

_____

_____

_____

_____

_____

_____

_____

_____

_____

_____

_____

_____

_____

_____

Harcourt Brace & Company

Industrial/Organizational Psychology

EXERCISE 98: Agree or disagree with the following statement and support your answer: 'Corporations and individual workers are natural adversaries. What is better for one is worse for the other.'

Critical thinkers avoid overgeneralizations. Is this statement, as written, accurate in some cases but inaccurate in others?

As you consider this statement, consider the nature of the needs of corporations and other organizations. What types of needs do workers have? Are they always incompatible? (Hint: What is the relationship between job satisfaction and productivity?)

_____

_____

_____

_____

_____

_____

_____

_____

_____

_____

_____

_____

_____

_____

_____

_____

_____

_____

Environmental Psychology

EXERCISE 99: Agree or disagree with the following statement and support your answer: 'Crowding people in together is aversive.'

If you picture the statement as referring to being wedged into a subway car with perspiring commuters on a July day, it seems true enough. But let us avoid over-simplification and weigh all the evidence. Do our situations (our reasons for being where we are) and our attitudes have much to do with our responses to crowding?

_____

_____

_____

_____

_____

_____

_____

_____

_____

_____

_____

_____

_____

_____

_____

_____

_____

_____

_____

_____

Harcourt Brace & Company

Name_____   Date_____

(Return to) Psychology as a Science

EXERCISE 100: Agree or disagree with the following statement and support your answer:
'It is possible to understand human behavior from a scientific perspective.'

Does this item sound familiar? It was the second statement in the exercises–following the statement that dealt with the basic definition of psychology. Now that you are nearing completion of your study of introductory psychology, has your response changed? If so, how?

_____

_____

_____

_____

_____

_____

_____

_____

_____

_____

_____

_____

_____

_____

_____

_____

_____

_____

_____

_____

Name_____   Date_____

_____

_____

_____

_____

_____

_____

_____

_____

_____

_____

_____

_____

_____

_____

_____

_____

_____

_____

_____

_____

_____

_____

_____

_____

Harcourt Brace & Company

Name_____   Date_____

_____
_____
_____
_____
_____
_____
_____
_____
_____
_____
_____
_____
_____
_____
_____
_____
_____
_____
_____
_____
_____
_____
_____
_____
_____
_____

Name_____   Date_____

_____
_____
_____
_____
_____
_____
_____
_____
_____
_____
_____
_____
_____
_____
_____
_____
_____
_____
_____
_____
_____
_____
_____
_____
_____
_____
_____

Name_____ Date_____

_____

_____

_____

_____

_____

_____

_____

_____

_____

_____

_____

_____

_____

_____

_____

_____

_____

_____

_____

_____

_____

_____

_____

_____

_____

_____

_____

_____

_____

_____

_____

Name_____ Date_____

_____

_____

_____

_____

_____

_____

_____

_____

_____

_____

_____

_____

_____

_____

_____

_____

_____

_____

_____

_____

_____

_____

_____

_____

_____

_____

_____

_____

_____

Harcourt Brace & Company

Name_____   Date_____

_____

_____

_____

_____

_____

_____

_____

_____

_____

_____

_____

_____

_____

_____

_____

_____

_____

_____

_____

_____

_____

_____

_____

_____

_____

_____

Name_____ Date_____

_____

_____

_____

_____

_____

_____

_____

_____

_____

_____

_____

_____

_____

_____

_____

_____

_____

_____

_____

_____

_____

_____

_____

_____

_____

_____

Harcourt Brace & Company

Name_____   Date_____

_____
_____
_____
_____
_____
_____
_____
_____
_____
_____
_____
_____
_____
_____
_____
_____
_____
_____
_____
_____
_____
_____
_____
_____

Name_____   Date_____

_____

_____

_____

_____

_____

_____

_____

_____

_____

_____

_____

_____

_____

_____

_____

_____

_____

_____

_____

_____

_____

_____

_____

_____

_____

_____

_____

_____

Harcourt Brace & Company

Name_____ Date_____

_____

_____

_____

_____

_____

_____

_____

_____

_____

_____

_____

_____

_____

_____

_____

_____

_____

_____

_____

_____

_____

_____

_____

Name_____   Date_____

_____

_____

_____

_____

_____

_____

_____

_____

_____

_____

_____

_____

_____

_____

_____

_____

_____

_____

_____

_____

_____

_____

_____

_____

_____

Name_____ Date_____

_____
_____
_____
_____
_____
_____
_____
_____
_____
_____
_____
_____
_____
_____
_____
_____
_____
_____
_____
_____
_____
_____
_____
_____
_____

Name_____ Date_____

_____

_____

_____

_____

_____

_____

_____

_____

_____

_____

_____

_____

_____

_____

_____

_____

_____

_____

_____

_____

_____

_____

_____

Harcourt Brace & Company

Name_____ Date_____

_____

_____

_____

_____

_____

_____

_____

_____

_____

_____

_____

_____

_____

_____

_____

_____

_____

_____

_____

_____

_____

_____

_____

_____

_____

_____

_____

Name_____   Date_____

_____
_____
_____
_____
_____
_____
_____
_____
_____
_____
_____
_____
_____
_____
_____
_____
_____
_____
_____
_____
_____
_____
_____
_____
_____

Harcourt Brace & Company

Name_____   Date_____

_____

_____

_____

_____

_____

_____

_____

_____

_____

_____

_____

_____

_____

_____

_____

_____

_____

_____

_____

_____

_____

_____

_____

_____

Name_____   Date_____

_____

_____

_____

_____

_____

_____

_____

_____

_____

_____

_____

_____

_____

_____

_____

_____

_____

_____

_____

_____

_____

_____

_____

Harcourt Brace & Company

Name_____   Date_____

_____

_____

_____

_____

_____

_____

_____

_____

_____

_____

_____

_____

_____

_____

_____

_____

_____

_____

_____

_____

_____

_____

_____

_____

_____

Name_____   Date_____

_____

_____

_____

_____

_____

_____

_____

_____

_____

_____

_____

_____

_____

_____

_____

_____

_____

_____

_____

_____

_____

_____

_____

_____

Harcourt Brace & Company

Name_____   Date_____

_____

_____

_____

_____

_____

_____

_____

_____

_____

_____

_____

_____

_____

_____

_____

_____

_____

_____

_____

_____

_____

Name_____   Date_____

_____

_____

_____

_____

_____

_____

_____

_____

_____

_____

_____

_____

_____

_____

_____

_____

_____

_____

_____

_____

_____

_____

_____

_____

Harcourt Brace & Company